Iota

Iota 90

Contacting Iota

Website: www.iotamagazine.co.uk
Editor: editor@iotamagazine.co.uk
Features: features@iotamagazine.co.uk
Listings: listings@iotamagazine.co.uk
Subscriptions: subs@iotamagazine.co.uk

Please send all correspondence and submissions to:
Iota
PO Box 7721
Matlock
DE4 9DD

Design & Layout:
Raphael Tassini & Andrea De Cal
Printed & Bound in India
Cover Image: ---------

Iota 90
ISBN 978-1-906285-13-5
ISSN 0266-2922   £6.50

www.iotamagazine.co.uk

Contents

Editorial Summer 2011

'There will be keening and caterwauling on an epic scale. 'Woe is us!' the corduroyed luvvies will chorus' reported Quentin Letts on the 30th of May in The Daily Mail. The day that Arts Council England announced their cuts to funding as a result of the government's spending review, austerity budget, response to the economic crisis, or ideological slash and burn, depending on your view.

So, was there 'keening and caterwauling on an epic scale'? Well, I wouldn't quite describe it like that. The day that everyone had been waiting for, like some twisted anti-Christmas, was young when the first announcement scanned up my Facebook page:

"We've been spared, phew. Good luck to everyone else.'

That was a theatre company. Then moments later:

'We are disappointed to announce that ACE have cut our entire budget. Thanks to everyone for all their support. Good luck to other organizations.'

That was a small poetry publisher. Then they started to come in thick and fast. Arc, cut. NAWE, cut. Enitharmon, cut. Poet in the City, new funding. Faber New Poets, new funding. Phoenix Dance, retained funding with a cut. Bristol Old Vic, funding saved. Northumberland Theatre Company, cut. Ledbury Poetry Festival, saved. Flambard Press, cut. And on and on it went. I was a bit dizzy and rather confused. It all felt so random and the 'results' were coming at such a pace it was hard to digest. I felt like I'd been assaulted with a series of slaps and kisses. Then came, Writers in Prison Network, cut. This felt like a punch in the stomach to me.

Having worked briefly in a prison I found the cut to the Writers in Prison Network astonishing. There is a wealth of evidence to support the usefulness of this organization. It is a known fact that literacy levels amongst prisoners are statistically very low. It is also known that children who have parents in prison suffer a decrease in literacy as a direct result of their parents' incarceration. To me it seems insanely obvious that writers working with prisoners to increase their literacy can only be a good and useful thing. Whether the use is in decreasing the likelihood that they will re-offend or if it means that they will now be able to write letters to their children while in jail, either way the benefits are blatant. What's more, ACE hasn't funded anything that will operate in its place. I suppose the problem lies in the Writers in Prison Network's 'client-base'. I can see that it must be hard to generate a 'sustainable income' from them. They don't earn much. We can't charge them.

Quentin Letts didn't need to worry. I mean, yes, there has been a response but it's definitely not 'caterwauling on an epic scale'. Facebook aside there was a mildly entertaining correspondence between a number of respected poets and Antonia Byatt of ACE in The Times letters pages. Carol Ann Duffy, Simon Armitage and George Szirtes amongst others asked ACE:

'…to reconsider their decision which will have a devastating impact on poets, publishers and, especially, on readers of contemporary poetry.'

Ms Byatt replied by pointing out that

'…we said tough choices would have to be made and that regretfully we would not be able to support some organizations…'

Tough choices? I think I've heard that somewhere before. My favourite retort came from Carol Ann Duffy a week later in The Guardian with her wonderful 'A Cut Back' written in direct response to the cuts.

> It's no go your poets in schools, it's no go your cultures.
> All we want is squeezed middles and stringent diets for vultures.

In the poem Duffy lists many of the organizations I mention above that received cuts. Duffy is more than happy to use her position to draw attention to the shocking cuts in art and culture through the medium of verse, demonstrating the relevance and currency that poetry can and does have in the 'real word'. 'A Cut Back', written after Louise MacNeice's politically charged 'Bagpipe Music', is witty, entertaining, accessible and clever. It is also complex. As complex as the reader wants to make it. Duffy takes her title as Laureate seriously and she writes for everyone.

The poem put me in mind of the Andrew Lansley Rap released earlier in the year. A collaboration between poet Robert Gee and rapper MC NxtGen, it's a response to the Health Secretary Andrew Lansley's proposed healthcare reforms. It became a Youtube hit and garnered quite a bit of media interest. Like Duffy's poem, it is witty, entertaining, accessible, clever and complex:

> It's all so you can save 20 billion quid
> to clear up a mess that the bankers deposited
> and now you're going to open up the NHS
> with sweeping reforms for which no one voted.

Like the Duffy poem also, it mentions specifics. Reading the lyrics you will see mention of Lansley flipping his second home and receiving payments from John Nash, chairman of Care UK a private healthcare provider.

These responses are not 'caterwauling'. These are measured, creative, informative and purposeful, artistic responses. And they do a much better job of making sense to me than many of the decisions being made at present.

So, dear readers, my call is simple. Keep writing, keep creating and keep informed. I have signed many petitions over recent weeks as the invitations arrive in my inbox, and I will continue to do so in the future. However, I will also still be reading, writing and trying to make sense of things. As more cuts, reforms and policies head our way I will be bracing myself. But I will also be hopeful that, as I reach for the next batch of Iota poetry submissions, I may just pull out another corking response to the situation. That I'll be entertained, enraged, and enlightened. They can't cut that.

Kate North
Reviews Editor

Poetry

Jane Commane

from *A Brace of Spinsters*

Our Lady of the Waiting

The past is no different,
they may say so, but she
is a winder and watcher of
numbers and knows better
than those who trust in anecdotes alone.

Opaque and safe as a corm
deep and corseted underground,
purled tightly as the lock of hair,
the filled tooth, the wedding ring
he planted in case she will grow again.

She knows the true clocks from false
and is only waiting to begin once more.

Moth Maidens

Not our topaz and amethyst relatives,
but pegged and pinned in stiff-collared
suits, we are all an array of dun and bronze
and modest in dust, mouse and fawn.
We are ourselves, and can only be this.

This will be our calling, vocation of moons
and of false moons, all stations of the crescent,
ours, the waxing and waning, the gibbous,
the milky full-fat clock face is our lighthouse-
lantern that guides our steps home.

Night is long and growing longer
but we mount up, lamp-lit and bold,
to haunt blunt towpaths, under bridges,
the dark at the heart of the road's
tar-black maw that opens up ahead

before the long silver pin
of November
through our hearts.

Our Lady of the Lost Surnames

You left her on the steps, out in the rain's christening
of a summer too early to care for cake-cutting
and picture-book photographs in a calf-skin album.
A forsaken relative neither invited nor remembered.

She took a black cab alone instead, through cleared
streets ringing with familiarity, the taxi meter tolling
up the long bill of wrong turns that had sent her
away on a scenic ride to a different churchyard.

As you signed her off one last time,
she was already in the earth, up to her knees,
burying each and every syllable of name
in the unforgiving flint and clay.

Our Lady of the Last-born

And all the world can turn by
in the spokes of a three-speed bicycle
that carries you here again,

under the gunnel that runs by the reservoir
and under the Oxford Canal,
she, your guardian

(I wouldn't say angel, no),
is there in the stubborn *tick-tick-tick*
of a Sturmey-Archer gear hub.

She who knows this small town
is too small, too narrow
and that it dislikes your dreaming,

thinks you should go back from whence
you came, and stop asking, wanting
for else or others.

For now, this late autumn evening,
fallen sycamore stars blotting
the spittling rain will make do, will mend,

and if you cannot sleep, troubled
not by what you have, but by
what you have chosen not to have,

think of this; the sight of meadows
by the industrial estate giving way
to Avon's sharp elbow,

or this town detaching
from the bloodshot retina
of sunset beyond the motorway.

The Pope and Saint Marx

Back then, every Catholic home possessed a picture of Pope John
XXIII. Some had lights that flashed, it was said,
to the rhythm of his heart. Most men in these households
were thankful for the light this cast which aided them
during the night to empty their weak bladders.

Mother's brother, Hugh, had two pictures, side by side:
one was the Pope, the other Saint Marx as Hugh called him.
Both were leaders of millions, he said. One was to assist us
into Heaven, the other to enable us to take what we were due
on Earth. This, the priest informed me at confession

was a mischievous notion. We prayed God would give me
extra guidance as I encountered such people as Hugh.

Owen Gallagher

On Behalf of the Dead

The living are constantly digging us up for forensic purposes,
to discover where things went wrong, for them, not us.
They haul us out of the grave when we are chatting

with neighbours, eavesdropping on visitors above, or in a deep
sleep. This can happen when they are on the loo
or have just finished sex; most often we are dragged

in front of the family and told how badly we let them down
or how poorly we brought them up.
When they are done, we make our way back to lie

in our graves and wait in turn for the grave-digger
to shovel the soil back on us, and ask him
to pack it hard, really hard, like cement.

Owen Gallagher

Listening to Angels at a Workshop on Earth

God does not believe in holding back floods,
or catching bullets as they leave their chambers.
Darwinian by nature, he supports
the survival of the slickest, depends on a surplus

of the poor. There is a backlog of prayers he is unable
to clear. He works closely with the police and has dismissed
petitions to create a parliament of angels.
He wears a bulletproof vest. No one suggests

retirement or a severance package. Heaven is full
of wiretaps. God's sons argue for a Republic.
He was last seen in the sky trailing a drip-feed on a trolley.

Owen Gallagher

In the Garden of Eden, Iraq

When I peer into the eyes
of Sergeant Farouk
I feel him curled up against me

at night, no longer the soldier
with notches on his rifle
who forces our regiment

to train barefoot in the red-hot sand,
but the one who brings grapes
at sunset, water and oil,

undoes the laces on my boots.

N7

I leave the pub alone,
zig-zag back

to the stench of Mrs Docker's
boiled cabbage in the hall,

to the stab of latch key,
to the rising tide

of dirty clothes and coffee cups,
to my arc leap

from door to bed
to sleep adrift

with a rescue cat so lonely
she purrs all night

in her seaweed hammock
of my hair.

Sheltering

I hide
under your window.

Wait outside
other people's half-cleared breakfast kitchens.

Breathe in
clouds of chalk dust left in an empty classroom.

Place mine inside
an off-pink handprint on a desk.

Relive one absent
kiss on the farthest reaches of my hair.

Silently a translucent leaf curls on the sill of a metal-framed window.

Mollusc

One filthy room, one naked bulb,
the pub then this. In my wall of mirrors

two bodies writhe: one big and red,
some headless horseman; the other,

just a slip. My face looks square,
shy smile scissored to panting lurcher.

Demon eyes stare, quite fixed,
as clean blade strikes in long pink

fingerprints. Soft white meat jerks
and rises, meets him, jiggling.

Ian McEwen

My Dishwasher Dialogues

My fridge either moans or is still,
the toaster can only ejaculate
but the dishwasher tells me a story.
It fills with welcome and hums while
it works. The sloppy cymbals syncopate
about the kitchen, keeping time for me.
Towards the end it turns a little
frantic, grinds about in the key of worry
before the gurgle down the drain
and one long steamy sigh. It sounds final,
the body cold and silent, PVC
and steel, but in the night again
it flashes green and ready,
   ready,
        ready for another cycle.

Fussing Kites

Now they are so common it is hard to feel much for them,
dropping in like airbuses or those things for parascending
or whatever weekend fashion for ascent will follow:
that has followed by now.

Yes, they are big and if not quite red, then rufus,
the handy colour of Australia, of big iron bones
on the beach, convincingly fossil and permanent,
but the annual count

holds no interest and all they do is hang around. We know
they are not killers. They grow fecund on allowances
of dog food, leftovers from Waitrose, and (as close to risk
as they get) the off-whiff

of ersatz carrion: the road-kill daubs
of nature levelled down. They have always been our fault,
not domestic or feral but public birds, eating the week's
dross, at medieval peaks

over the crap-strewn cities, the largest, and above
all London, not second home but the umbilicus
for their carpetbagging population. Look up: pinned flat
onto the sky like tat,

repro-crucifixions, watching each suburban food-stop,
out of reach, impossible to shoo off.

Possess

There's a girl living
   beneath the floorboards   I only catch
glimpses of—
     her thin hands   thick black hair
collect shadow   In the attic room I wait

      days weeks   years pass
she's here tonight
   arriving up through the boards
eyes filled with moonlight
         a finger to her lips
         a hand on my shoulder

      she tells me secrets I cannot
 speak of   pushes me down
onto piles of soft clothes   duvets
        kisses my eyelids shut
        then once on the lips

           hovers over me until I don't
know myself   till I think
      myself ghost   She slides back

into the floor   leaving my skin
      salted from her kiss
         new and sharp within me as stars
as the haunt of her voice
      calling me after her

Dried Mango

Sunlight through the windscreen
and she's beside me

salty and sweet
the pull of my car around curves
gospel choir singing   *Midnight Train to Georgia*

She takes each strip out
holds it up to the sun
names the shapes
one by one
like the first naming of things
— foetus   labia   seaweed —

until each takes on life
and we dangle them above our hungry mouths
goldfish-orange
slow ripeness
opening
With the juice
a rush of hidden words
I chew mine   careful

not to crush the ones I need to say
—sister   desire   home—
whole heart in my mouth

First Diving Lesson

It's all in the hips, you tell me—

        the kick of knees locked
hip-joints cresting in one long tail-flip
        all muscle   pushing water.

I try it   float upwards   try again
     but it's only when you swim on
        I feel this pull   then dive

sliding belly along the bottom   twisting round
     until I'm beneath you   twinned
        green-gold scales

this watery light. Your fingers
     pale and webbed reach out   touch
        the curve and edge of me

a drum of air beneath skin
     my song ears—you
        draw me in.

Sleepzone Hostel, Connemara

A Korean woman mumbles
in her sleep, a language like
the jangling of keys. The German

in the bunk below jerks the whole bed
with her dream, our blue metal frame
a ship-hold in the dark. By day break

they're up: brushing teeth, taking turns
in the push-button shower. For all
the sounds in the night, today they exchange

no word, move like cats, stepping sideways
to let another pass. From my bed I know
each one by her careful tread—scuff

of shower shoes on tile, boot heel clack
across the hall, a barefoot plod over boards.
These strangers I've slept among all week,

names ungiven, destinations unknown, just
the being together in this place,
each of us travelling alone.

Luigi Coppola

The Morse Code Boy

After the tongs and tug
the blood tapping from the ear
he was born to a two tone world

The dot - pinch, prick,
bite, stab, the needle
through the eye

And the dash - the skid mark,
smear, stitches, the ka-smack!
of a follow through fist
the slide of a knife
around a wrist

Home was a chessboard
streets a jazz club
school a blotted note
the syllables and spit
black and blue on white

So passing the yellow line
of a grey platform, the long and short
stride of a light through smoke
takes him through that last grinding dash
all the way to a slowly blinking,
shrinking, distant dot.

Autograph of a Thief

With a wrist whip he'd split a safe
With a finger wring a lock
Even his stare could seep through walls

A kind of royal magic, he sang while he stole
Serenading each sleight of hand

I asked him to find a wordsearch
Within a crossword hidden in a game of sudoku
All locked in a liar proof box

It was like watching a cocoon crack,
A pearl expand or an eagle pierce the wind
And then the windpipe of a house mouse

After, as a receipt, he wrote a puzzle
Out of his name and I handed over payment

At parties I show off his anagram autograph
To anyone that believes in stardust
Whoever works it out I'll marry

At the Pool

Patterns of light you only get
in open air swimming pools
shake and bend over themselves
in the slow lane.

Two girls say hello, smile too wide.
Plump seals call, disrupt all the lanes
having as much fun as they can,
(bubbles in the shadows)

with their clothes on.
I'm careful to smile back,
breast stroke past them
through a world upside down.

One girl takes off her shorts, hides
them behind her back, the other
shuts her eyes and counts, then screams
and pretends to look for them.

I duck away under the rope. Water snorts
up my nose, floods get everywhere.
I glance downward into refracted sun,
to check she's still got her bikini on.

Other fingers scatter surfaces.
She's having a laugh, her friend
spouts water upward like a whale.
Spiders of flickering light nest on our faces.

Marion Tracy

The Giant

Lake Wakatipu, South Island, New Zealand

I'm trapped in a toy coach going down a mountain.
There's a lot of hair in the forest (and fingers).
White petals look up at me.
I'm the small one.
We're all desperate for sleep, anything
to escape from the coach driver
also from kilometres and too much geology.
The giant, Matau, seduced the chief's daughter
and was burnt to death as he slept:
punished into landscape.
His burning body made this giant hole.
The window smells of nothing (help me please)
I can't hear a heart beat in this lake.
Trees avalanche; gaps shine like missing teeth.
If he's still here, his belly full
of melted mountain, he must be
lying down, curled up on his side,
as if still sleeping.

Grammatical Second Person Talks Back

Had it up to here with being you, everyone
wants a piece of me, writing about me, giving instructions.
It's, you do this, you think this, you do that,
you feel this, so over it with epiphanies, swallowing
ego is becoming increasingly uncomfortable, not as authentic
as in my youth. After years of angst, my amygdala
is like a whore's whatsit, if you get my meaning.
Guess it's been a full life, travelled a bit, but time
to put all that behind me, go into recovery
get a few people off my back, find my own glass slipper,
swan in my duckling, flesh in my wooden
puppet moment, no forwarding address.
Tried cloning myself, franchising the concept but success
just meant more meetings, so here's a substitute
for you to interview, maybe not totally satisfactory,
not as inclusive as me, less likely to be mistaken
for fiction, not much presence, very short
but from my point of view, it likes to be first
to take its clothes off in public and that's
the person spec in a nutshell.

Marion Tracy

Tree

You talk of the sea
but give me a tree, any day.

Tree stands upright like me,
has arms like a man.

Sea has no limbs or shape,
lies flat like the earth.

Tree knows how to grow old and die.
I'm not afraid of a tree.

Sea retreats and then comes nearer,
will drown me if it can.

Tree is a sign of hope.
In the wood I am given shelter.

Sea has no religion,
by the tide I am knocked over.

Tree is worthy of worship,
hangs bright green buds and leaves.

Sea is empty of meaning,
breaks apart frail shells and bones.

In The Hilton Hotel

I left my heart in the Hilton Hotel,
a cherry bomb throb in a twist
of night-wound sheets.

Other trips had been distinguished by loss;
the credit card in Prague, missed when gin
infused tonic at 20000 feet,

Dad's slim gold watch, sunk into the dust
of 4000 guests behind a bedside lamp, the ring,
still on a dish when I handed back the key;

unintended tips and gratuities, found in the wake
of hung over departures, kept by those
on scant wages.

My wife noticed a pallor and torpor as she greeted me.
Later, when she laid her ear to the vacant room
of my chest, the game was up for good.

Telepathy

In an old address book I found you,
migrating through a list of struck out streets,
from your mum's house to halls of residence,

to that room above a bakers, where a three bar
heater raised steam from your knickers
and damp made wallpaper blister.

We never made it to the age of touch-scroll,
the up-lit glow of lone faces on the night bus;
for us, rendezvous were arranged in advance,

our love not text fed, but kept hungry by absence,
when timetables were lensed in rain and dying batteries
dragged music away under the stations steel rafters.

One night, as we spoke on the corridor payphone
where even queens had to queue, your voice let slip
that you had left me, but I already knew.

Roy Marshall

Ghost Walk

New apartments by the factory weir;
here, the fat freckled kid throws a pound note
into the river to watch another boy swim.

Wind whipped cherry saplings in the park
are fully grown, flaunting handfuls of blossom.
The witch's hat has left a stain of iron.

An air-raid shelter deep in leaves, fear of rats,
a nudie magazine; all now under house foundations.
Set the bell ringing above the door of Tommy Allen's sweets.

Mum, beautiful, aloof, blowing a *'once in a blue moon'*
plume of smoke. Who to be today; Zorro, The Flashing blade
Robin Hood?

Silas's Funeral

…the best bit
was the Lawrence poem which spoke about
things men had made

and I remembered
   the craft of your carpenters hands

patina of your life
   in the warmth of wood

sheen and shape of the tables
   cabinets and chairs

those lovely things
   which will live on…

Denise Bennett

The Child

after The Toys by Coventry Patmore

His dead mother, who was patient
would not have hit him for disobedience
but used reason or kind words.

He missed her tender ways,
her soft breast, her smile, her kiss;
the bedtime ritual of filling
the treasure box together with toys:
his counters, his shells, a red-veined stone,
beach-worn shard of glass,
a bottle with bluebells, his two French copper coins.

Late into the night he could still feel
the red rose on his wet cheek,
hear his father sobbing.

Denise Bennett

June

Innumerable bees are fumbling
fingerstall foxgloves;
skimming sweet williams,
the crepe skirts of paper-thin poppies
can-canning along the path.
I hear the descant of a thrush,
smell the fragrance of lavender.

Under the apple boughs
on the lawn, a small girl
in a pink gingham dress dances;
a wildness of summer in her limbs
as she skips and spins,
the wind catching the full blown
peony of her skirt.

Denise Bennett

Hatch

Found On Henry V111 warship Mary Rose which sank in 1545

I was found in bits by divers
and taken from the *Mary Rose*;
pieced together, like a kit, bone

by bone, thigh, spine, skull, shin;
a ninety nine percent skeleton,
except for some missing teeth and toes.

Discovered beside the carpenter's cabin,
they have named me *Hatch,*
tell how I used to catch rats.

I'm the oldest sea-dog in the land,
not some ancient, salty sailor,
jolly Jack-Tar with weathered face,

but a dog in a brave a new place —
Henry's bitch preserved in a glass case.

Denise Bennett

Washdays

In those days housewives
were marked out
by the whiteness of their linen.

So much depended upon
the copper under the drainer
screened behind the red-check curtain,

the way my mother
hauled it out and heated it up
on Mondays;

her arms in bracelets of suds
scrubbing weekly stains
with bars of soap;

snowy white ropes
of sheets she twisted into the sink;
skimming shirts from the creamy surf,

and me, her dark-haired girl,
biggest secret of her life,
scurrying like a rigger

to help her carry the basket,
help her hoist the spotless sails
over the pre-fab garden.

Cradle

She said he'd a knack with small creatures.
A grasshopper stilled on a kitchen tile
would risk the gathering cradle of his hands,
the trapped bird repeating its bruised error
on rattled greenhouse glass let him
unlatch the way, the moth that, flustered
by light on the landing, abandoned
the skimmed bedroom ceiling, arc back
to settle on his wrist, rest suddenly slack
then poise to launch upon blackness. All
could be calmed, it seemed, their dusted
feet welcome on the soft heel of his palm
could be raised, could be released to fly
ascending unbounded to the opened sky.

Pedigree

Out of Balinagask Jock and Thovey Bank Susan
the best birth certificate in the family spanned
four generations of Mactavish pedigree, fountain penned
in 'forties permanent black, sire and dam,

Malgens, Sandleys, Heathers, Sheilas, number one
in the stud book, whelped, certified, no ration
for him, unlike my briefer blood line,
cardboard identity stamped for National Registration,

no erasure or alteration on pain of fine or prison,
not to be parted with to any other person,
produced on demand to an authority in uniform,
removals notified to the Officer, brown, under sixteen

ensured proper portion, in the drawer in the kitchen
with the other cards, vaccination, divvy, dad's army pension.
I fold them into each other, one by one, for protection,
his then mine then mum's then dad's, the back of mine

signed by parent or guardian. But Angus had none
when he slipped unseen, unheard, into that pond,
struggled and barked for hours before he drowned,
her wedding present gone, until the delivery of a son.

The Old Wife

At last, we come to houses
where the human has receded,
leaving totems on the shore,
wrecked cargo from the tide -

a table not a table, but
driftwood in the dust sea of the room;
the room has lost its function,
is now a cave for swifts

The door flaps and screeches,
at night mutters, quite senile
Inside, the light is rotten,
no one home; except

in the gappy jaw of the cellar window
she has left 3 bowls stained rust
for the inevitable cats, all feather-mouthed,
selfish household gods
attending our decay

Sarah Davies

Tabula Rasa

i

When I can't see to write,
I go around the garden with my regulation piece of paper,
hold it against:

the half dead tree -
white buddleia alive, drugged bees

the rough hide of the flagstones -
a chalk rainbow washed off

my bare leg –
golden hairs, indigo bruise

the sky –
a massive frame of blue

this window cut
out where I hold the paper up,
making all things smaller so they fit
onto the blank sheet, describing it

ii

Dad's painting of the park at night,
the trees diagonal with the push
push, of the world outside the frame,
two owlfaced people watching from the secret garden;
at least that's what Dad painted, murmurs,
listen – or, if you won't,
then place the paper mute across it, hush

iii

What are you drawing?

I'm drawing
a window

What's in the window?
Night and a girl
What's the girl doing?

The girl in the window at night
is painting
a picture
What picture is she painting?

She's painting a picture of a girl in a window
at night, painting
a girl in a window, painting the night
and this girl in the window painting
a window with a girl painting

the night with a girl in a window
is painting the girl. Look very carefully,
see - in the last painting,
the girl at night in the dark window
is opening a door in the painting's side -
tearing into the light. All this paper's white.

David Duncombe

Missing

After she left,
he slapped the double leather photo frame
faces down on the emptied cabinet,
stared now and then at the tarnished brass clips,
the soft creased hinge and *Modern Studios*
stamped in flaking gold, a business long-gone.

He had plucked out the monochrome strangers,
to fix their own new poses in their place
like captured butterflies, forever young
and side by side, while they had grown older
and apart, forgetting the need to smile.

Long after she left,
his pain had faded into a vague past,
but a in desk he thought he'd cleared, he found
an envelope with her name, this address,
the letter missing, the stamp and postmark
from a time, a country, he'd never known
and he wondered who she was, this woman,
her wardrobe bare, the clothes hangers undraped.

At last he picked it up, the frame, gripped it
face to face, unclipped the prints and ripped them,
halves and quarters, binned them, mingled now,
and set the faceless frame standing again.

David Duncombe

Friday the 13th

A black cat pads across my path
and I check my step but carelessly tread
on a crack between the paving slabs:
old superstitions, those pointless games
we play with tea leaves, ladders, scissors, salt,
filling the gaps in our same-old days.

Yet real bad luck drops in to stop your world,
shaking the random to knock you down:
police at your door, hats on for crime,
or off for the news you always fear.

It alarms you with a phone call in the night.
It lengthens the silence as your chances slip,
face to face, after you risk, 'I love you.'

There are amulets, crosses, charms,
calming prayers and verses, placebos all,
so throw them back at the holy men.
You'll find them on both sides intoning
their blessings before a war they'll never fight.

And If politicians in tailored suits
tell you how to cut your cloth, you won't need
a crystal ball to see hard times ahead.

As for the bookies and odds against,
to lose your last twenty on a horse that falls,
is not bad luck, if all the others
on your card cantered too slowly home.

Let me just dodge the bullet, the deviant gene,
the worst things you know; I'll chance crossed knives,
the ace of spades, the claptrap count to thirteen.

The Warp of it

Shadows play across the wall; chimneys
rise out of green linoleum. Three floors below
a fire hydrant gushes; kids yell. Summer's electric soup
floods the studio. The artist has become a lightning-rod.
The painting twists. Orange-verdigris slashed
through a cosmos turned building-site
is lost in black. Scaffolding collapses.
A glass of scotch slips –

              Unbidden the brush
hurls a bolt of tar; out of the vortex forks
two strokes. Verticals, cross-bars align. Something
matt and blue catches, dips. The canvas
has become a giant sign,

a calligraph of August's heat and grime, this
stifling night, this life –

              (a slim cat leaps after
       a brown-armoured whirling thing; knocks down
        a pair of jars; bats; damages a wing)

Neon-white streaks off a palette knife.

X-ray

Good clean photo, man.
The technician waves a slide. His teeth gleam.
Thanks, Sam.

My father frowns
as he takes in the alien leg. *A piece of meat.*
He shakes his head.

Is he thinking of Goya? Hospital gown,
wall, sheets on the bed
planes – spare

as light;
we are pinned on a screen, all breaks
and twists of darkness

bare:
and the strange bare fact
that I am here beyond pained years.

His hair is white, soft,
no longer the grey wire he scissor-chopped before
the narrow glass

in the windowless hall:
when he rebuilt the loft, his paintings
got the light.

Those luminous canvasses locked away – *City on Water,*
Dancer, Une Histoire Triste,
The Hostess

with scarlet lips, high waltzing heels, and garter.
The man with
pink bow-tie and one blue sock who is

Trying To Walk On Water.

The Snowdrop Growers

We appear in the bulb books,
possessing the chromosome for snowdrops;
moving Jiffy pots round the garden
after the sun. We have the knack
with FRAGILE bags when the bulbs arrive,
weeding with nail clippers and cocktail sticks.
Nature wastes nothing, plastic, rubber, tin,
spitting on its hands, taking a fresh hold,
appearing in Lowry's long wedding,
glad to hear voices in the house once more.

The Carpets

A wonder they have any shape at all
sliced up, trimmed down, stuck together on all fours
to fit four homes in a dozen years.

But here's an alcove, a square of hearth
and the fourfold dents of the TV plinth.
Design hasn't left completely yet;

a couple of strides and we're somewhere else
dragged up and scissored out, tufted and ruffled
where the children fought and the kazoo group played.

Here's the stove, no simmer control,
maiming and scorching a Rorschach blot
into lino; castor-marks made by an armchair

hammered together with tintacs
and sinking beyond repair into the floor.
There are doormats we trample, bang and dust

from bedroom, kitchen and junk space;
the hoover cutting round a square of carpet
infinite, frayed and tiny.

The Whoosh

Swiped from a car, a radio needs the freezer;
nestling in the ice-box, the key code breaks
and you switch it on, the brilliance unimpaired.
Too little's been said about the sound
as things erase from history; secret codes,
car number plates that drop from sight,
a re-sprayed motorbike running round town
or things chucked away like bendy wire
for breaking into vans, the Styrofoam coffee cups
that listen through a wall
at the bodiless voices of the neighbours.
Think of the hairgrip that never lets you down;
the tiny click, a brief god opening a Chubb,
and that collection, a freezer full of radios
among the luncheon meat and tomatoes,
the high-amp socket that restores the whoosh.

Best Before

The kitchen is the last room to clear.
I reach up. From her top cupboard
I remove illegible ageing jars
as someone leaves. The front door catches.

On the once white plastic shelving
sticky crime scene outlines tell
tales of spills, leaks and slow drippings,
lids not screwed on tight enough.

I excavate. I start to scrape
at labels of spice long past its best
Half empty, unfulfilled condiments,
furry, far too foreign, at the back.

I take the sink by surprise, force feed it
the exotic. And each neglected ingredient
joins a carnival, whirls for an instant, releases
its own desperate aroma, before being washed away.

The First Wife's Skin Cells

He made this wooden bed for you and him,
romancing your poverty. Pride seeps
from the structure. Spring sap. I have built
my fine nest high. New stains map the mattress
where my waters broke. Yet beneath me
your skin cells cluster in the joints,
settle deep in the grain where discarded hair
burrows the cracks of a creaking frame,
calibrated by your rhythm. I listen
to descendants of dust mites fattened
on the stuff of your sediment and sweat.
I could clone you from this bed,
resurrect you just to prove that it is me
he wants. That is why I do not let him burn it.

Helen Reid

My Father's Beard

Because today my hand shakes
less than his, I am to shave my father.
So squeezed between bath and basin,
cupping awkward chin I scrape
at a beard grown wild and strange,
as long as the days since she died.
Just once he flinches and swears.
Now squeezed against a cabinet, jammed
with drugs and sharps still to be got rid of,
I work the other side, recalling how
I would recoil from his embrace and jerk away
a tender cheek, avoid a graze. I run
a hand against the grain. "That's better,"
we both say, as I rinse away the evidence.

Helen Reid

Exile

Even so, I stay at the guest house where
in an atmosphere thick with other souls
and brassica, I lie on a single mattress made
slippery with plastic protection, in a room
with a view of the dawn or the dusk painted
by numbers, nailed to the wall, hung over
my head. Though a room lies empty elsewhere,
here are ornaments to wonder at: a bowl
of dust and dead buds freshened up by a spray,
peach perhaps; a grimy shepherdess standing dainty
guard over teabags and powdered milk in tupperware .
And when the dawn chorus of expanding pipes reaches
its thermostatic climax, I will send out a signal,
a teaspoon, tapped, repeated, on the radiator.

Breaking

Breaking news: a woman's let her tea go cold.
A bulletin. She weeps. Do we have sound?
And the family of the soldier has been told.

It's official. Of the hundred who were polled
ninety five percent agree she should be proud.
Back to the scene. Yes, the woman's tea's still cold.

We will keep you posted as events unfold.
Now the weather. In the flooding all hopes drowned
for the family of the soldier who've been told.

We've just heard that he was twenty one years old.
It's so tragic; next the value of the pound.
Join our phone in. What's your take on tea gone cold?

Now the virtue of the boy must be extolled
for his body, even now, is homeward bound
to the family of the soldier who've been told.

Just to recap then, with him they broke the mould.
Though his blood's still warm in distant desert ground
yet our experts can confirm her tea is cold
and the family of the soldier has been told.

Decree Nisi

Kelly, this week I've filled the house with strange men:
the plumbers and plasterers, the 'leccys and lackeys,
the lofty young shifters and shifty old lifters,
the chippies and butties, the world and his mate.
The cash-in-hand, the big white van
blocking natural light to the living room.
The painters in white overalls, the strip
they wear when drinking tea for England.

Kelly, this week I've filled the house with strange things.
Stepladders and handshakes, buckets with holes in:
I make a wish and throw the hourly rate in.
The settee's on the lawn, a madman's garden swing,
paint brushes take up leg room in the sock drawer
and a hammer sneaks in with the knives and forks.
A photo of your mother's face down in the toilet;
dust sheets make ghosts of the tables and sideboard.

At ten to five they call it a day,
promise to be here bright and early.
I abracadabra the TV from under our old bed sheet,
settle down to a plate of leftover digestives.
It's then, Kel,
when the stars come out in the curtainless windows
and the telly echoes through my home.
It's then I say your name.

Restaurant Where I am the Maitre D' and the Chef is my Unconscious

I put through an order for fettucine al oglio.
He sends out a soup-bowl full of blue emulsion.
A regular asks for lamb shank with rosemary.
Out comes a beetroot served with a corkscrew.
A man I suspect of being a restaurant reviewer
orders the chocolate fondant pudding.
A mermaid rides a horse out of the kitchen.

He locks himself in there for days.
All I get are incoherent mumblings,
often in French. Some nights after closing time,
we sit down together with a bottle of wine,
get on famously, see eye-to-eye.
Next morning he sits in a deckchair all through service,
wearing a paper hat and a vicar's surplice.

'That's it,' I say, 'I'm speaking to the owner.'
That night, he shakes me awake,
takes the lid off a serving dish:
an actual star he's taken out of the sky
and put on a plate. I know it's only a dream,
but next evening at the restaurant I'm bright and early,
shouting the orders, shaking the customers' hands,

picking bits of gold out of my teeth.

Sleeping in Elephant Print Bedclothes

I never hear
his bookish tread or feel
walls of warm air flapping
from the ragged edges of his ears.

He wears across his back
the secrets of the Thar,
an invisible howdah high above
the continent of his belly.

Sometimes I'll glimpse a foot
the girth of a tree-stump
retreating from the outer edges of
my subconscious plains,

or while arguing with a composite
of close family members
I'll see dusty-lashed eyes gazing
back at me with solemn curiosity.

Occasionally I awake
the next morning with a leaden head
and the strange sensation
that my nose was longer in the night,

so long that I could spray
the quenching waters of distant oases
over my parched desert skin
while playing in the sand with the antelope.

But most of the time he keeps
himself to himself
and the only sign of him on waking
is his footprint deep in my pillow.

Navigation

She scores my breast in black felt tip:
X marks the spot —

as if my body were a treasure map
where a buccaneer could flip his fortune
with a stash of diamonds, rubies, bullion.

Or, arriving too late, unearth
rocks, coal, fool's gold
with which to fill his pockets

before leaping from a flapping
skull and crossbones

                into sapphires.

*

Daubing India ink, she pricks
my breast three times —
nipple, scar, sternum:

beauty spots, she smiles.

Later I sponge away the blue stains
and examine it, my Bermuda Triangle:
a zone in the western North Atlantic
where anything, even pleasure cruisers

can disappear.

*

Every day I break the line
of infrared, take up my position –
knees raised, arm stirruped above
my head, head keeled left.

A motor whirrs and I'm fed
backwards into a red objective;
reflected in the glass plate: my breast
harpooned by light.

The buzzer strains and flashes, invisible darts
target the beached blubber
of my organ – numb, swollen, scarred –

as if it still showed signs of life.

Robin MacKenzie

Interior with a Young Violinist

After a painting by Gerrit Dou

Light falls on a hemisphere
of my old globe, on to the score
I played from just a moment past.
Notes hang in the velvet air
until they're cancelled by the dust.

A pewter pot lies on the floor,
a book with heavy covers casts
its shadow, teasing me to find
some meaning in the randomness
of my half-lit interior.

Practising in my attic room
I animate this little world
of silk shiver and metal gleam,
dull leather and tawny wood.
Behind me, steps lead to a darkened door.

Robin MacKenzie

My Heart at Twilight
After Georg Trakl

At dusk you hear the bats squeaking.
Two black horses frisk in a meadow.
A red-leafed maple is rustling.
There's a tavern up ahead on the road,
where delicious nuts and wine are waiting.
Delicious too your drunken swaying
in the twilight wood. Through the black branches
sad bells sound. Dew falls on your brow.

Caroline Natzler

From the Light

And now, under the weight of dusk,
peering out at dim homes and trees that hardly hold up

though above the rubble of next door's works
a white canopy lifts with a flourish
left over from before the dark
from the field-tents of kings who wore their crowns into battle,
from pastures dappled with miniature deer
and girls in silk let down from the light,
the slanting of a flute from the hills
and frogs in the stream, heaving calls from their bellies
the day a scaly, burning creature pricked you as we lay

as we lay in a sun we'd never known but always knew was possible,
and the landowner turned out to be English, in a Range Rover
come to restore the olive groves, he said
      - for paradise, we thought.

Do you remember? How long will you remember?

Cycle

Raggle-taggle of flesh and mind
weary of always plotting
for each next moment to come right

you long for stillness, the one
word beyond narrative, to resolve

the muddle and shiftiness of time
nudging on night after night
and the always going down of things

until, as if by birdsong rattling in the dark,
you are roused, sense how the scramble of words
and the opening of moment into moment

bring abundance, a curious, dappled living

and the sun rising like a story.

Jake Campbell

Marsden

> 'If we don't know what England is, or what made us, or what we value, then how do we know what to retain, protect and develop?'
>
> Paul Kingsworth — *Real England*

I look out over a tinfoil surf
imagining the colliers, sailing
Marsden's black diamonds
down England's spine.

Below Souter Lighthouse,
now National Trust stamped,
fields grafted on the periphery
of cliffs are a betrayal

of topography. Down here,
where the secrets of the Bay
smugglers still whispers
through shells, we forget

the village that vanished.
Membranes of coast folding
into a totality of sea; the drifting
away of old industry.

The grinding pebbles still tap
like the rapper and the purl
of shore curls like the Rattler,
but all ages osmose

to mythologies, are cast
flat under fields,
into a finality of maps;
negatives; folk-tales.

The Fall

itself was no more accidental
than an envelope slipping
down the back of a radiator. Cliff-side
of a denim sky, the other dog started
circling, nostrils to the wind.

Stomach to grass by this point,
my uncle shimmied on elbows
beneath the 'Danger!' sign
to confirm the pup dead
in his yolk of blood.

Seeing his tail threshing
some sixty feet below, he rummaged
down Trow Point over pebbles, cracking
as snapping celery. Twisting his ankle
on a runway of seaweed, he howled
on to fetch the crazy little fucker.

Paddling his hands
under the stomach and hind legs,
the tongue flapping
like a leaf caught in an extractor fan,
the shivering animal must've felt
brittle as a satin pouch of marbles.

The climb back to land-level
was surely the first time
he'd had to hope
never to be forced to carry
a child this way, log-legged and moist.

Seeing the 309 at the end of the Leas
gave him conviction to run.
By the time he'd reached the vet,
the old curtain he'd wrapped the dog
in showed only a petal of blood.

Jake Campbell

When the surgeon told him to shut up
with the story; it was crucial they operated
immediately, that he should inform the owner,
he sat in the car park, engine ticking over,
chain-smoking Regal.
He took a solitary black hair from the edge
of the passenger seat and rolled it till
his fingers ached.

37 Morpeth Avenue

Time has boiled away leaving behind its salt of memory. On the blackboard,
our names still etched in violet and peppermint. The homemade measuring
chart on the doorframe shows Robbie at 87 cm in Jul. '98. The last marking,
Jan. '99: me, 128 cm. Across the hall, Dad's old room still smells of 1973.
Of FA cup glory, Subbuteo men still in their boxes. We fear peeping into
Granddad's bedroom, the way we did while, downstairs, Granny whisked
eggs, ironed blazers. The same purple wallpaper, quaver-curled now, droops
above the pile of railway magazines, the glass head with its hat of hair and
the bed sheets, like a skin of milk, ruffled as if not twelve hours earlier, two
figures tussled in the night. In these rooms, where the sun has stubbed out
its light and spiders have flown slick, silk kites, we retrace the preface of our
lives, still visible as finger-drawn names, outlined in the years old dirt of the
pane. Talking about the dead is easy, they can't argue back. Perhaps that's why
we want to see what happened in '86, when Dad vomited onto *The Gazette*,
hurled it to the corrugated roof of the garage below, pigeons beginning to
circle. We want to see him down a pint of water and 3 aspirin, do up his 30
inch corduroys, buttoned with the settee stud; watch him apologise to his
parents; tell them he's going to his girlfriend's. We want to see what our
grandparents meant by that glint in his eye.

Heredity as Seen Through an Eight Inch Mirror With a Disposable Razorblade

Irises hitchhiking the mirror's cosmos of spots,
I lifted Dad's Gillette from its pool of rinse.
Streaks of stubble protruded from the blades
like docked centipedes' legs.

I foamed my face, held the reflection
in my left, the razor in my right.
Took a deep breath,
recited maxims
to do with following
the growth of the whiskers.

The pulse in my neck quickened
as I pressed the rectangle
to the exploding firework of my chin,
fantasised about girls stroking
my cheeks, punctuated
by maturity's angled sideburn.

Came out the bathroom with Andrex
tassels held on pins of blood.
Besides the 37 hairs I counted
using the magnifying
side of the glass, my face remained
a strip of mud awaiting its delivery of turf.

And as I glide his Fusion Power
down the crest of my cheek ten years later,
still uncertain of my technique,
I could blame Bics bought from late-night garages
off the M62, bristles hastily chopped
in Formule1s outside Bradford,

but patrimonial knack can hit a dead track
for reasons less prosaic than the service stations
in which it was forgotten.
In the darting of our pinball pupils,
we omit as often as we forget:

what punishment might result from an E in Maths;
whether palettes of de-icer and batteries
would still shift in the warming of ball-binding air;
the opposite wish – a thaw, for an easy trundle,
taking Westoe R.F.C to Llandudno.

Knowing the four-day-old scuzz of hairs on the sink
were the last to ruffle between his mother's
chemotherapy wig as, four days earlier
he cuddled her and she said, 'Oh, I'm fine,
but you need a shave.'

Learning to Surf at Night

Stitched-up in a cat-lick of borrowed skin,
I'm harpooned by the body-nearness of it all —
cold penetrating the inner coils of heat.

The sea bangs me up against the girders
of the old life boat station;
eyelids and ankles trampled

by semaphore waves
like the white-flagged hills of Cappadocia
breaking into a stampede.

I volunteered for this —
my muscles clench:
baby fists raising the spinal rig
until I'm up, vertical

on hell-hound shoulders,
and un-seen stepping-off points.

The Black Dog Bagel Shop

The crutches are her leverage:
she's strong as twin swans –
only slow at lift-off.
She spreads mayo;
his skin warms up like fat tomatoes.

She's an island wreathed
in steam, dispensing
clouds of cinnamon
as he clicks his teeth:
it's the daily riff –
it's *Mornin' Country* on the radio.

She never talks about her injuries,
whips up cream, spreads almond butter and dill,
re-fills jars of coffee beans.

He switches from super-mild
to double strength Brazilian.
Spooning demerara sugar, he spills it
over the table top and ducks,
waiting for everything she's got.

Losing You at the Beginning

1

The program for your funeral
is displayed on the mantelpiece,
like the invitation to our wedding –
but with my name missing.

We had a winter honeymoon
in Lyme Regis, climbing
up and down molehill paths –
you, looking out to sea.

We got dug in.
You built a tunnel to escape
my hard diamond-mining
will to find you.

2

It could never last:
the perishing smiles, the tiredness
at the corner of your mouth.

Me and our children laughing
in the freezing night, watching
shooting stars over Portsdown.

3

Instead of love, I remember
the picturesque:

Me holding a handful of earth
to fill
the hollow in your body.

Slivers of ice from the branch
above us fall, pockmark
your skin, your perfect limbs.

Interviews

Matt Merritt

Matt Merritt is a poet and wildlife journalist from Leicester. His most recent collection, *hydrodaktulopsychicharmonica*, was published in 2010 by Nine Arches Press, following *Troy Town* (Arrowhead Press, 2008) and *Making The Most Of The Light* (HappenStance, 2005). He studied history at Newcastle University, and his current project is a poem and photo sequence inspired by the Midlands Revolt of 2007. He is a co-editor of *Poets On Fire*, and blogs at: http://polyolbion.blogspot.com

Interview by Angela France

I am greatly enjoying your latest book, 'hydrodaktulopsychicharmonica'; the poems are fresh, precise, and varied. One phrase in particular stayed with me and seems to me to be something about your process: 'A tinnitus of distant/ guessed-at lives' ('January'). Is this where some poems start for you? With 'guessed-at lives'?

Yes, I think that's very frequently where poems start to take shape. I'm very suspicious of being too consistently autobiographical, if only because like a great many poets, I suppose, I really haven't led a very interesting life. Of course personal experience does find its way in there too, whether in the details or the emotion that drives the poem, but it's very rare that it provides the initial spark, I think. It all means that I'm constantly looking elsewhere for inspiration, and I generally think it's more exciting as a writer (and a reader, I hope) to start from a fairly brief glimpse and let imagination take hold. I'm afraid I'm always glancing into lamplit living-rooms when I'm out walking, or scribbling down snatches of conversation overheard on the bus - poetry is a perfect excuse to be downright nosy.

What happens after the 'brief glimpse'? Does it immediately become a poem? Can you describe your process from that point?

Generally I work fairly slowly. When I started, I used to write down every idea, line or whatever the moment I had it, but although I'm still one for carrying notebooks and scraps of paper about my person at all times, I tend to be a bit more relaxed about things these days. I have to drive quite a lot for work, and I also spend a lot of time walking, so over maybe two to three weeks after the initial idea I try to write nothing down and just turn stuff over in my head while I'm traveling. If it sticks, it's worth persevering with. After that, I usually work through several drafts, although sometimes I write two or more drafts in parallel, heading in very different directions. Having said all that, very occasionally I'll write something very quickly straight from that moment of inspiration, and not revise much at all. It doesn't seem to happen with any particular style of poem, or subject matter, though, so I suspect that it's usually something I actually have been turning over in my mind without realising it.

You mention driving for work which gives you thinking time and I know you work as a wildlife journalist; how does writing for work impact on your poetry writing? Is it difficult to 'switch gear'?

I do find it increasingly hard to switch from one to the other, so if I'm working from home, for example, I tend to get up really early and get the day job out of the way as soon as possible so that I might feel like working on some poetry by early evening. I used to work on newspapers, and then for various trade journals, and at that time I found the switching between the two rather easier, perhaps because the sort of writing I was doing at work was more technical, or straightforwardly factual. Now, even a lot of the writing for work has a certain creative element to it, so perhaps that's why it's harder to separate the two.

Having said all that, I can't think of many day jobs that would be easier to combine with poetry. It involves plenty of time on my own, and it's fairly easy to schedule work around writing poetry, or readings, or whatever. There's also a fair amount of crossover, because a lot of my poetry concerns the natural world, so here have been quite a few occasions on which research for work has led eventually to a poem.

Finally, on the rare occasions that inspiration strikes while I'm at my desk, it is nice to be able to break off what I'm doing and scribble something down without anyone batting an eyelid!

As you say, the natural world is present in a lot of your poetry – but also cities and towns; the city as glass harmonica, the town as a conduit to history. History seems to be woven throughout this collection: not as retellings of textbook history but examinations of the nature of history, the interweaving of public and personal histories. Why poetry? What can poetry do in examining history that other forms can't?

That's a great question!
I think poetry's own marginal position makes it a good fit with some of the more obscure areas of history. Poetry ought to give a voice,

or voices, to outsiders, and that's often who we're talking about, history being written by the winners and all that.

But it's often the case that these hidden histories only come down to us in the first place because of poetry - popular poetry. Robin Hood, who crops up in the book in the guise of Roger Godberd, is a good example, but there are others. It's the same with things like the little snippets of natural history folklore in the book - in a lot of cases, they've been remembered thus far because they've been preserved in poetry or song.

There's also the fact that all the best stories in mainstream history have already been told over and over, so prying into some of the darker corners is your best chance of finding something new.

Do you go 'prying into some of the darker corners' with the writing of poetry in mind or do you find those hidden histories first, and the discover the poems in them ?

It's usually been a bit of both. When I started, I think I was rather shy of doing too much 'research' of any kind for a poem, because I think I had the rather romantic notion that they should spring, fully-formed, entirely from some secret source. These days, I'd have no problem with deliberately seeking out historical scenarios that might produce poetry. Having said that, though, I think I more often find the hidden histories first. Other than when I was doing my degree, I've never been at all systematic about studying history, so there are huge gaps in my knowledge, but I do read an awful lot of it, so I'm always coming across little triggers for the imagination. And I think it goes back to what I was saying earlier about the start of a poem - if I'm reading a history book and something or someone in it keeps nagging away at my mind, I'll let it do so for a while. If it sticks, I start to think there might be something worth writing about.

So, after an idea has been 'nagging

away' at you for a while, and you decide it could be a poem – how do you go on from that point? Do you complete a draft at one sitting? Or work at it over a period of time? Are there any particular conditions you need to write – silence, music, a window?

It's very rare that I write a poem in one sitting, although I think it has happened a handful of times. More often it takes me weeks, sometimes months or even years, because I revise and redraft a lot, and quite often now write different drafts in parallel. There are at least two poems in the new book, hydrodaktulopsychicharmonica, that started out 7 or 8 years ago, around the time I was writing the poems that ended up in my first chapbook. They're unrecognisable from the way they were then, but it takes a lot to convince me to discard something in its entirety. I recycle all sorts of scraps here and there.

I think I can write in most conditions at a pinch - in the past I've certainly scribbled drafts while on the bus, or at work - but I prefer to work in my living room, in the evening and late at night. Music's a definite no-no, because I find myself slipping too easily into the rhythms of whatever I'm listening to, but I don't really work well with silence either. If it's quiet and peaceful, I tend to start looking for distractions, whereas if there's some fairly undemanding, low level distraction already there (cricket on the radio or TV is a favourite), I get far more done. I can dip into or out of it whenever I need a minute or two away from the poem. I know it's not really a recommended way or working, but I was exactly the same at school.

Do you use other readers as any part of your revision process; workshops, for instance, or trusted friends?

When I started, and up to the publication of my first chapbook, I used an online workshop a lot. There were lots of good writers on there, from all over the world, and it was a

huge help. Unfortunately it all seemed to peter out, so since then input from outside has been a bit more sporadic, but there are a couple of poems in the book which came directly out of one-off workshop events. For the most part, though, I didn't workshop poems or show them to friends as I went along, other than by reading some of them at open mics (and they're not always a great guide to what will work on the page).

I do like to get a lot of feedback on the finished manuscript, though. Poets James W Wood, Matthew Stewart and Lizzy Dening read it for me, as did Tom Bailey, a photographer I work with, so I had a bit of perspective from the point of view of a poetry reader (but not writer). Matt Nunn and Jane Commane at Nine Arches also worked really closely with me on the MS - I like that sort of editorial input.

You mention workshopping online; how much impact does the internet have on you as a poet?

I think it probably has a huge impact. Not in the sense that I've made good use of it for collaboration, or anything like that (although I do think it offers a lot in that area), but definitely in how it allows you to learn from and respond to a much wider range of poets than would otherwise be the case. I read lots of poetry online (although I often end up printing it out to read away from the screen), and of course it makes it so much easier to get hold of less well-known names in book form. Because of irregular work hours and commuting, too, I've always found it hard to get to the same workshop or poetry group on a regular basis, so the internet definitely plays a part in helping me feel like I'm part of a wider poetry community.

I'm really intrigued to see how poetry e-books are going to develop in the next few years. I think when they first appeared there were inevitably problems, but a lot of them seem to be getting ironed out. I've seen a couple of great examples lately and I think it offers all sorts of possibilities.

You clearly enjoy unusual words; the title *hydrodaktulopsychicharmonica,* **and** *Uchronie* **as a section heading and poem title are not words in everyday currency. Do you find unusual words trigger poems – or do you seek out such words to fit already-written poems ?**

Yes, I think unusual words definitely trigger poems for me. I've never really sought them out, and certainly not for a poem that already exists, but I do find myself jotting down anything unusual, or that sounds particularly different. I'd guess this might be one of the areas in which the internet is affecting poetry, in that you can come across a word, and within a few minutes have not only the meaning but also an enormous amount of background information and context for it - whether that inhibits the imagination a bit, though, I'm not sure. I'm a bit paranoid about giving too much credence to something I've just seen online, so I tend to go away and do some old-fashioned ferreting around in libraries.

Finally, what's next? Are you conscious of the next collection?

I am, and I have a couple of ideas that I really want to pursue in it, but having said that it's all in the very early stages and I'm quite prepared for everything to take off in a completely different direction. I don't have any timetable for it, either. At the moment, there's a couple of particular forms I'd like to explore in a sequence rooted in Welsh mythology, and there's a sequence that's inspired by a number of writers on the environment.
Quite separate from all that, I've been collaborating with Tom Bailey, the photographer I mentioned earlier, on a chapbook-length sequence called Goosepastures, about the Midlands Revolt of 1607 and the man who led it, Captain Pouch, who managed to be heroic and pathetic at the

same time. We're in the process of tweaking a few last things, but where we'll go from there I'm not sure. It's hard to find a publisher interested in a book that involves photos, so we're looking at a possible e-book format, maybe with sound files too.

Flashes

The tired earth has given way
and black water accumulates
in gullies and pools that change
week to week, day to day;
your memory's map instantly obsolete.

*

Forget the family forest trails,
the new-builds, the retail park;
to us it's always the village where
no one remembered the first spark
but fires always burned beneath our feet.

*

We are riddled with memory.
The hollow hills, the sleeping towns,
the shifting streets resonant
with what's been taken out.
We are rotten with history.

*

Scrape away the accumulation
of years. Here's what they hauled up.
A hardness that still hangs on
under the fingernails. A darkness
that escaped through the bars of the cage.

*
\

A conversation into the dark. An ongoing
exchange that yet yields a little light,
a distant heat. Unquantifiable pressures
do their interminable work
even as the unrecorded past subsides.

Sundays In May

Something should be starting. While you breakfast
slowly on the leavings of the week, watching
fledglings scream their demands across the lawn,

the seeds of an idea should be reaching
for the surface. Watching the trees making free
with their confetti, your heart should be surrendering

to the unlearned salmon leaps of love. You should
be seeing clouds not as rain but as the opening
of a wide, white country before astonished eyes.

Your song should be earning the blackbird's praise.
Walking that avenue into town, passing students
dragging bags to the laundry, revision notes tucked

inside the News of the World, you should be moving
towards something that has waited for you
all your life. If it is to happen,

here among the ice-cream vans,
the two-for-ones and the pavement tables,
it's as well that it should happen soon.

Waitress in Taos

Not the nights, as you might suppose, not the
nights without want or hope, nor the start of the day
alone between one thing and another

but somewhere in the heart of the afternoon
when piecing it together is like trying to remember
where the clouds were the same time an hour ago,

then, and only then, for comfort he pictures her
still working as a waitress in Taos, serving killer chilli
and margaritas, sleeping six hours, tops, but so well

that the bedclothes look almost untouched,
dressing by the glow of last night's embers,
a nearby streetlight, the big old radio

then out into the wide, euphoric air
with the sharp, ascetic thrill of an empty stomach
and the chill of a morning, thin and rare

but thickening with the scent of piñon smoke,
waiting for that point in late afternoon
after the last of the lunchtime tourists

but before the first of the homeward drinkers
when she'll step through the open kitchen door
and watch the ice-blue lens of the sky

bring the twinkling lights of the strip closer
to dance and play like some strung-out flotilla
easing its way back into harbour.

Michael Symmons Roberts

Michael Symmons Roberts was born in 1963 in Preston, Lancashire, UK.
His 4th book of poetry –*Corpus* – was the winner of the 2004 Whitbread Poetry Award, and was shortlisted for the TS Eliot Prize, the Forward Prize for best collection, and the Griffin International Prize. He has received major awards from the Arts Council and the Society of Authors.

His continuing collaboration with composer James MacMillan has led to two BBC Proms choral commissions, song cycles, music theatre works and operas for the Royal Opera House, Scottish Opera, Boston Lyric Opera and Welsh National Opera. Their WNO commission – 'The Sacrifice' – won the RPS Award for opera.

His broadcast work includes 'A Fearful Symmetry' - for Radio 4 - which won the Sandford St Martin Prize, and 'Last Words' commissioned by Radio 4 to mark the first anniversary of 9/11. He has published two novels, and is Professor of Poetry at Manchester Metropolitan University.

Interview by Vicky Paine

You've written several poems in response to the Human Genome Project - why does it interest you so much?

I had a day job up to about ten years ago as a documentary maker and during that period I worked on a series called *Science Friction* for BBC 2. It was an attempt to look at cutting edge science and the moral and political issues it was raising and whether society was addressing them properly. During the course of this film I was sent to The Sanger Centre in Cambridge where John Sulston was heading the team that was mapping the genome. I was very powerfully struck by this for a number of reasons. One was just the spectacle of it:

when you walked into the building there was a receptionist sitting at the desk and above her head there was one of those - they're like electronic ticker tape that you see on buildings in America with temperature readings - it was a live gene feed going across: as the computers were crunching the human genome it was going live on to the internet. I thought it was such an extraordinary image. And then in the interview with John Sulston I was very struck by the poetic beauty of the gene map: how these four letters, A, C, T and G, were all that made the difference between us and a salamander or an oak tree. It was just an extraordinary idea and I know I'm far from being the only person, or the only artist, to have been struck by that. Bits of the imagery then started creeping into my work.

Was it a conscious thing?

At first not, it just had a big impact and then it started to creep in. Then around the time I was starting the early work for the fourth collection [*Corpus*, (Jonathan Cape, 2004)] two things happened. One was that I started to notice that the collection was shaping itself around images of the body. I got the title quite early on, *Corpus*, and decided I would make that conscious and try to write a book that explored that as fully as I could. Then there was an opportunity to meet John Sulston again which came about through John Burnside and Maurice Riordan commissioning a poem for their anthology *Wild Reckoning*. When I was asked which scientist I would like to meet, I said John Sulston - I'd always remembered my encounter with him. Since then they'd finished the mapping and I thought I'd love to find out what was happening, so I met him again, and a number of things had changed. One the things that had changed was that Sulston's moral fervour was now directed towards campaigning against gene patenting. The poem, 'To John Donne' was directly responding to what Sulston saw as the outrage of gene patenting. The other thing that came out of that meeting was it got me thinking about how the metaphors were beginning to become accepted and were seeping out into the culture. I suppose the central metaphor cluster is around landscape, topography and mapping. That seems to be widely accepted now; John Sulston was very aware of this and interested in its impact. I owe a tremendous amount to him and felt very privileged to be there, first as a filmmaker and then as a poet. I haven't been able to leave it alone since.

How have scientists reacted to your work?

I gave a reading a while ago in Newcastle and there was a geneticist there. I'd read 'Mapping the Genome' from *Corpus*, which is about the miles of dead code [code that doesn't seem to have a function]. The geneticist came up to me afterwards and said "Actually it might not be dead – I'm sorry, that ruins your poem doesn't it?" And I said "Actually it doesn't at all." I'm not doing a systematic job of reflecting contemporary genetics, I'm actually plundering it for new ways of exploring my set of questions and concerns about what we are, what the body is, what the relation between us and our bodies might be. So as far as I'm concerned (plundering is probably putting it a bit strong) I feel no compunction or difficulty about drawing on theological language to explore that in poems, and scientific language also seems to me an infinitely powerful way of doing this. Something like the metaphor of us containing dead code seems to me so rich that even if it transpires in ten years' time that none of it's dead, I'm still glad the poem's there. I wouldn't consciously lie about the science I'm reading and trying to understand, but I also don't feel a moral responsibility to keep up with the science.

If people don't read poetry for information, how is scientific knowledge functioning in a poem? And if a poet does get it wrong, doesn't it in some way ruin the poem or take away from its integrity?

I suppose there are moral responsibilities not to create a poem that is wilfully getting the science badly wrong. But a poet like John Donne, one of my great heroes, his work is full of what we would now regard as junk science, but it doesn't matter; poets were using what they had to hand, whether it's the landscape or the relationships they were a part of, the science they were exposed to, the books they read. It's all part of – did Sylvia Plath call it "the store"? – a store from which you can then draw, to try make sense of what you're trying to make sense of in your work.

There is a distinction between the co-opting of scientific language into a poem and the exploration of scientific ideas alongside political ideas and, in my case, theological and philosophical ideas. It's got to be more than just the language co-opted to add a bit of potency; I'm not very interested in doing that. I also would never think myself as someone who "writes about science"; it never feels like it's that way round. I mean every poem in *Corpus* is about the body and it draws on ideas from all those different fields that we are currently using to try and understand the body. But I've never yet thought "I must write about genomics". Science isn't a subject for me; it's a method, it's a set of ideas, it's truth-seeking fundamentally in the way that theology is. And I'm interested in it as a tool for truth-seeking and therefore as a way of looking at the real subjects.

Can you talk a bit more about why you chose John Donne as the person to write this poem about gene patenting to?

A number of reasons. One, just personal taste – I love John Donne's poetry and he's always been a big influence on me. Another is that he is someone who connects different spheres of metaphor and brings them together to explore one central purpose or idea. So in the same poem he'll have theological language, scientific language and the language of erotic love. I like that and that's sort of what I'm trying to do in some way. Also as soon as John Sulston said gene patenting is like common land that's being appropriated I thought, he's talking about the body as a landscape that can be explored, defended, attacked, appropriated, and that just made me think about the poem 'To His Mistress, Going to Bed' and the extraordinary set of images about his new found land, his America. And also John Donne is interesting because he is someone who was probably among the last generations of poets who could be abreast of the science of his time and the theology of his time and equally learned and passionate about both. And he was also a poet, it seems to me, concerned with truth-seeking in poetry.

Although Corpus especially is very concentrated on the physical world, obviously you're very interested in the soul and in 'The Box' you talk about despite having someone's DNA, still "all the lights and currents of his soul are lost to us". How do you fit genetic mapping together with the idea that we have souls?

One of the obsessions of my work is what does self mean? And part of that is what does soul mean? I don't believe it's a ghost in the machine. I don't believe the phrase "I love my body" or "I hate my body" has any meaning: there's no differentiation. To that extent I don't believe in the soul as a sort of essence that floats off. My thinking in this is: I think and hope, rooted in the Judeo-Christian philosophical tradition, that if there is a next life, which is possible, again as explored in *Corpus*, then it would be physical, it would be corporeal. Now, how that operates, how you get your head around that, is a whole other question.

Going back to your original question, what drew me to genetics? I think a lot of my work is concerned with the body and the self and

where identity resides, so it fed into that. But what's fascinating about it is that I do think genetics as a science is extraordinarily beautiful and complex and fascinating, but it's still told us remarkably little about ourselves. That's the other thing that interests me, there's a contrast – and 'The Box' relates to this – when the genome was being mapped, newspapers were writing things like "This is our own secret identity being revealed to us" and yet when it's revealed we're none the wiser. And actually it's not because we're laypeople: scientists are none-the-wiser about this too. What it's informed us about is the huge complex web of probabilities. That's basically what it's told us - that depending on the way your particular gene code is cast, there is slighter greater probabilities of X or Y, or less, but there are still large parts of the genome that are not properly understood, the function isn't properly understood, the way that different parts interact are not properly understood; it's still intrinsically mysterious.

I get the impression you don't have any difficulties reconciling scientific theories with your own faith.

No.

Or is it more complicated than that?

No, it's not complicated, it's just that I don't see them as mutually exclusive in any way. I met a lot of scientists and a lot of religious thinkers over the years, not least when I was making documentaries for the BBC when those were my kind of subject matters. I met a huge number of scientists who had personal faith; I met a huge number of people who were professionally involved with religious thought who had a scientific training and background. It seems to me they're not at opposite ends of the street from each other, they're actually very close. And the impulse behind them both is almost identical. Both fields I think, are driven forward by **people who aren't just prepared to go out, work, eat,** and go to bed. That impulse to say why, what's this for, what's going on here, what does it mean to be me, what does it mean to be you, how do we interact? leads you into the practise of science or philosophical theology. I don't see any distinction, I've always been interested in both.

Returning to metaphor, you've talked on other occasions about the language being "up for grabs" and metaphors being "hammered out" at a time when the genome was being mapped. It makes it sound a bit arbitrary.

I think it is a bit arbitrary. Science is very rigorous in all sorts of ways but it seems to be quite haphazard in the way metaphors become accepted. I think most science doesn't proceed linguistically, most science is either non-linguistic or pre-linguistic and genomics is no different from that. But as soon as a scientist comes out from the first experiment they run and tell another scientist what they've been doing, or they tell their partner what they've been doing, they're using metaphor, because they're having to frame something that's non-linguistic, in language. I'd love to know when the first attachment of mapping to the genome was, because it could have been something completely different - it could have been drilling, it could have been a downward movement. At some point someone has said "we're mapping the genome" and then from that a lot of other things follow and a whole world of landscape imagery arises and now almost all discourse about genetics is based on that. Around the time that I met John Sulston, mapping the genome was already widely accepted but not much else was in terms of the computer genome: what it was, how you would look at it, what was it like to be a geneticist who was mapping the genome. I was there saying to John Sulston: What does it feel like? What do you feel like you're doing when you're doing this? He said "I don't know, it's like…" He was trying to…plucking things… trying to explain what it…Because it's not

linguistic and there's no committee - The Royal Society don't have eminent scientists sitting round saying "I think we're going to use the landscape metaphorical field for this." Scientists say things, they get published, one metaphor leads to another cluster of metaphors which broadens it.

Can I ask you about the two poems called 'Mapping the Genome'? One was in Raising Sparks which was published at the end of the nineties. And then you wrote another one for Corpus and deliberately chose the same title. Did you want them to be twinned in the reader's mind, to make that connection, or was it just for your own interest, developing the ideas?

I thought they were linked and therefore I was happy for that thread to be drawn between the two of them, but I also thought it was absolutely the right title for both of them. The first poem is using the idea of mapping the genome as a metaphor for knowing someone in the sense of a loving or sexual relationship, and the biblical sense of knowing someone. I was interested in that knowledge of someone becoming not just psychological but physical and, at the time, the mapping of the genome was just beginning and seemed to me to have some of those properties of an almost sacred quest to get to know someone as deeply as possible. At the time we didn't know what this gene map was going to amount to. So then later in *Corpus* when I was very overtly writing about the body again, and these genetic ideas were coming through more and more, I thought I need to return to this. Because actually my sense of the mapping of the genome was changing, there's a slightly different sense of it, but it's also a different perspective. The first poem is, I suppose, a love poem, which experiments with having a scientific metaphor above it. So if you write this love poem and then you preface it with a title like 'Mapping the Genome' what does that make you see differently about the tenderness that's being played out there? Does it make it more manipulative, or does it make it more profound or beautiful? I was interested in that chemistry. By the time I came to write the second 'Mapping the Genome' poem I had this awareness that there was still a lot of untrodden snow out there in terms of the metaphors for genomics. And that was why I thought: Hey, there's not much been written yet by poets or novelists about mapping the genome and what it might mean to be the person doing it. So I thought, you know, driving through a desert, let's go with that.

I suppose the thing about poetry is, if it's foregrounding the metaphors, then it can take these metaphors and re-open them and allow us to consider how they're shaping the scientific ideas.

Yes, exactly. It's about foregrounding and renewing metaphors, making them conscious again. But what's interesting is even dead metaphors can have an impact. So the fact that we call a cell "a cell" may no longer seem to us like a metaphor, but there are all kinds of subtle ways in which that influences the way we see our own bodies and the way in which other kinds of science affects our bodies. For example, cancer, - and this shades into Susan Sontag's view on medical science and metaphor - the whole metaphorical structure of cancer as being military, using military metaphors. So metaphors can still be active even when they're dead.

Zombie Metaphors!

[Laughs] Yes that's right, exactly! I'm fascinated by that. And trying to make conscious and explore metaphors for the body is what I was trying to do in *Corpus*.

I'm interested in not just how poetry responds to scientific ideas, but how poetry affects other discourses, including scientific. It's very difficult to quantify – well, it's impossible, but

just the fact that poets are sensitive to these sorts of etymologies and play with them, I do feel that it shapes how we think about things, even if it's in a completely unconscious way.

It's hard to think, because of the marginal condition of poetry in society at the moment, that there's a regular or direct influence of the one on the other. But if poetry is, as I would argue, our culture's most focused and advanced work on metaphor – at its best, that's what poetry is – then that has effects. How you trace them is another thing. A poem or a metaphor in a poem strikes someone else who's writing in another medium or gets picked up by a journalist or gets mentioned in a conversation… these things are then viral aren't they? But I do think, although you can't trace the line, there must be an impact. Once you get a really complex, multifaceted metaphor like the body as a city, or a piece of landscape which can therefore be defended or attacked and so on, which is a massive metaphor structure at the heart of all medical science and popular discourse, well, yes where does that come from? What's the role of poetry in that? I think it's probably quite significant. And if you interpret poetry broadly enough to go back to some of the founding poems of our culture, like the Psalms when they were first in English, I think it's unarguable that they had a shaping effect.

Can poetry ever be said to have a function?

Broadly speaking, not in the sense that function would normally mean an active and generally acknowledged role in society in the way that books have a function – no, not in that direct sense. But in another sense, yes, and it relates to metaphor and science actually. Poetry is not by any means the only sphere in which we use metaphor - metaphor is everything we say - but poetry is one of the few places where metaphor is foregrounded rather than backgrounded, where metaphors are chosen and teased out and renewed and argued over. And therefore, at its best, poetry is the most heightened, intense and painstaking use of metaphor we have in the language. And if it is that, then there's something important going on there. If, for example, a field like science (but politics as well) uses metaphor largely unconsciously, in my view, but *constantly*, and if you believe, as I do, that metaphor is enactive in the way we respond to things, it's not just illustrative, then of course it's important.

Do you ever worry that poetry is so marginalised, that even though the poets are teasing out these metaphors, and thinking about how they're shaping the way we think, that that's not having any impact anywhere else?

Yes, this is a huge debate. I would love it if everybody who read the next Ian McEwan novel would also read the next Seamus Heaney collection but society doesn't work like that. I think it's partly because of the way we read and the expectations we have of reading now. I'm not one of those people who think we're on the verge of a great poetry resurgence. I think there's fantastic poetry being written but there's no evidence that it's going to become the new rock 'n' roll, the new anything else. I suppose I am slightly pessimistic about it. But I think poetry tends to stick around so you might not have breadth but you may have depth. It may just keep going and it's probably the one form of writing where it's quite possible that a poem that really encapsulates something for somebody might still be tucked away in a drawer for a hundred and fifty, two hundred years. And even in a society that has largely rejected poetry I think it's still not completely been secularised, it's still regarded, in an unspoken way, as a faintly sacred form of art in a way that actually, no other form of art is. I wrote and presented a radio programme about elegy for Radio 3 last year and one of the things I was arguing on that was: why don't people tend to read extracts from novels or scripts from Eastenders at funerals? It just won't do, it's not good enough. The language isn't doing what you want it to do. At times like that, only poetry will do.

Reviews

Speaking Without Tongues
Jane Monson
Cinnamon Press, £7.99

Speaking Without Tongues is Jane Monson's first poetry collection and an essential read for those interested in contemporary prose poetry. Each poem in this collection offers a meditation on the title in what has been called by Helen Ivory ' a sparkling, eye-opening debut'.

Rather like William Carlos Williams' assertion that there are 'no ideas but in things', Monson's *Speaking Without Tongues* demonstrates the impact of the physical world on our use of language. Further more, Monson meditates on the seeming impossibility of language at times where the physical world appears to operate in place of it. In the opening poem 'Church Falls' Monson delivers a closing stanza that serves to illustrate the redundancy and also the necessity of language:

> 'A marble falls from the pocket of a boy and tells us where the rug ends and the stone begins; he lifts another to his smile and swallows it, tugs at his mother's sleeve. Tugs again.'

It is in this terrain that the poet must always operate, the space in between the physical and the expressed is the smelting pot or the furnace where the poet creates. The image of the child replacing speech with a physical object put me in mind of Gertrude Stein's insistence that the poet should be concerned with nouns and the naming of things. Rather than naming the object in Monson's poem the child consumes it and then looks to his mother for a response. This is a strong image that represents the position of the poet in many respects.

Variances of this image reoccur throughout the collection. In 'Hunger' a female protagonist 'picks a pebble from her last tide-line and swallows it whole'. In 'Little Sisyphus' an ant carrying rocks is described as 'speaking all day in stone'

This uncomfortable association between mouth and stone is elaborated with lines that demonstrate the unease of speech as in 'The Clock' where we are told 'In a minute, a thought will leave his mouth by accident' or in 'Peter's Pica' with 'Peter's mouth is always being watched'.

In many ways this is a collection that centres on the idea that as poets and writers we are forced to reacquire language each time we confront the blank page. Monson's poetry navigates the difficulty of this but also celebrates the wonder of the process. In the title poem 'Speaking Without Tongues' Monson orchestrates the internal world of a train carriage alongside the external countryside view. The worlds are seemingly separate, each posited by the other as a backdrop to its own existence. However, Monson ends with the line 'By night, their conversation twins in the dark' showing us that the poet's place is alive in facilitating communication where once there was supposed none.

The tone of the collection builds up to a feeling of expectation as the images of frustrated speech give way to a sense of freedom in language. In 'The Speaking Cloth' Monson declares 'As her throat fills with the wind and the flowers, she hears the sun, ticking carefully over her head.' Here Monson is showing us the sense of achievement and happiness that comes with the expression of emotion through language. Here the natural world, the wind and flowers in the throat, display the power of language and it's very interconnectedness with the world it attempts to describe. At once this collection becomes a celebration of language and its relation to the physical world around us.

In the closing poem 'Visible Speech' Monson describes the burning of turf in a fireplace:

'Once lit, these packed cuts of land, ease themselves away in smoke;
return themselves to the earth in powder'.

Here Monson uses the image to illustrate the impact that our use of language has on the physical environment. The 'tongue of the chimney conducts' the smoke back outside. This, in turn, demonstrates that both the physical world and expressions of it through language are dependent on each other.

This is a collection that I keep returning to. To me it speaks about the very concerns we all have as poets when attempting to fit language and our impressions of the world together into a space called a poem. I'm already excited about what Monson is going to show us next.

Kate North

Hydrodaktulopsychicharmonica
Matt Merritt
Nine Arches Press, £9.00

The opening poem of any collection not only sets the mood, but sets the bar for the level of quality throughout the book, and the first poem in the first section of this collection, 'English Literature', is a fantastically concise and apt opener. The 'I' of the poem has their pen held over 'the gaping permafrost/of the page', the movement of the trees outside is a 'slow, emphatic argument', and the final stanza reads '[O]ne chance, you get at this,/he is telling us this from the front,/One chance'. Writers are often inclined to write about their craft, and the tradition that sits heavily on their shoulders, and this is one of the best I've read. Merritt takes his chance and keeps the level of quality in the next hundred or so pages at a consistently high level.

It's apparent in this book that there has been a long and patient consideration, for not only the semantic possibilities of the directions in each poem, but the sonic qualities of each line, and how it eases the movement of the stanzas. 'Glass' explores the idea of words as crystallised objects, here Merritt beautifully links terminology between the two topics with description such as '[F]rosted, smoked, stained, caught in a beam/for an instant, they collect, then separate, light', ending with the final lines 'they're always on the point of breaking. That much is clear'. This piece is a brilliant example of the well balanced alliteration of the book, but also, the way Merrit manages to find a new approach on each topic, without falling into cliché. I didn't get the feeling at any point that he was treading on the shared territory of other poets, regardless of the familiarity of the content.

In 'January', there are some beautifully original descriptions as the character in the poem passes 'joggers and dog-walkers' as he follows a trail up a hill, their passing a 'tinnitus of distant/ guessed-at lives'. The sight of the stars explored in the 'feel of their long-dead light/unseaming your aching spine, already bowed/by their terrible weight.' The natural landscape in many of these poems is something best showcased in 'Swifts', a nine section piece where the poet changes from a more traditional use of form, to one where we see lines broken and cascading across the page as content reflects form.

Not all the pieces here reflect the local landscape of the poet, or the wildlife that inhabit it. There is a real rarity in this collection; a brilliant, cohesive list poem, with a depth of feeling. Every line is a stand-out in 'Things Left in Hotel Rooms', some of the highlights being '[T]he shape of troubled sleep, cooling/and hardening in the unmade bed' and '[T]he ghosts/of Saturday night. Scattered like fox-kill across the floor'. Smiles and grimaces are 'stranded on the shelf/ in the bathroom' and excuses are '[T]hreadbare, glad of the company'. It's a poem that shows off the strength of Merritt throughout the book; the concise and original similes, the tight, easy language, and the thoughtful use of form.

Whilst reading *Hydrodaktulopsychicharmonica* I was reminded in places of John Burnside's stark lines on nature, as well as Robin Robertson's beautifully balanced ambiguity of language, but Merritt has forged his own style in this collection. His dedication to craft is evident throughout the book; each piece is paired down and polished, and not only does this make the book a joy to read, it made me excited with expectation of future collections from this very assured and original voice.

Dan Sluman

The Night Post: A New Selection
Matthhew Sweeney
Salt, £12.99

One of the second wave Irish poets, Matthew Sweeney has an impressive output of over twenty collections since 1981, through a diverse range of publishers that includes Faber, and Jonathan Cape. *The Night Post* represents a new selection of his work, including the unpublished *Moonpoems*, as well as selections from *The Flying Spring Onion, Fatso in the Red Suit, A Smell of Fish,* and new, unpublished pieces.

The first sixteen poems of the collection focus on a thematic interest with everything lunar. In poems such as 'Visit', we encounter some of Sweeney's consistent tropes in the casual, almost note-like simplicity of diction in lines such as 'I fight my way upsteps, /find wind in angry mood' . This journalistic, present tense tone combines with elements of the supernatural and a nod towards magic realism in the end of the poem, where Sweeney searches for an apartment at night; '…27, 26, /…but where, / WHERE/is 25…?'.

In 'Drought' there are some fantastically concise and aphoristic lines, such as 'rain has suicided/from uselessness'. Sweeney also demonizes the sun in favour of the moon, and lacking in water, claims 'I've even tried my blood/but sadly/there's no future there.' But for each time Sweeney finds a new angle on a well-wrought subject, he also falls into unredeemable cliché, such as 'the night invades. /The reign of darkness is back' in 'Nightfall'. There is also an undue amount of repetition and tame metaphor in some of these poems, an example of the latter in 'Winter'; 'I am no polarbear, disguised as snow. /I am not even tough. Coat a useless bodyguard'. After reading the first section of this book, I was surprised by the lack of originality and force in many of the lines, but held off further opinion until I had read the rest of the text, attributing the criticisms mentioned so far due to a lack of scope in the topic of the *Moonpoems*.

Outside of this section, there is plenty of accurate and innovative imagery in poems like 'ZZZZ'. In this dynamically formed piece, Sweeney continues his process of concentrating on the minutiae of a moment, in this case, trying not to fall asleep. With lines such as '[B]etter that/than a scimitar on the sleeping skull, /a silencerclad luger/whistling through my teeth', this mundane territory is made exciting through alliterative ease and fresh imagery, Sweeney narrowing his poetic eye to the point where everything described is in the process of flux.

It is not just the originality and clarity of image that are the highlights in this collection though, in 'Neighbourly Sounds' we encounter Sweeney waking to the sound of a neighbour reaching orgasm. The humour found in her noises and her lover acting 'as if trying to sell his function/to all the street's women' helps to break the tension of taboo, whilst the ending of 'and just then/I notice dawn has come' provides a fitting cadence to the comedic tone of the poem.

In other pieces, however, Sweeney's judgement on whether he can make something fresh out of the mundane is positively skewed. In 'The Flying Spring Onion', the first three lines are as such '[T]he flying spring onion/flew through the air/over to where'. Besides the Pam Ayres'esque end-rhyme of 'air/where', the lack of delicacy in the language choice exhibited by repeating the title as the first line and then compounding this with the same verb (flying/flew) stunned me, especially in comparison to the other work described. He does this again in 'The Sleeping Sailor', the second to fourth lines being 'lay a sailor. /He wasn't dead, only sleeping-/sleeping off a night of rum.' Perhaps I am more sensitive to such clustered repetition than most readers, but in using the same verb twice in as many lines, I'm left wondering whether something new and enlightening could have been used in its place.

When Sweeney does move away from the everyday to a topic charged with stronger social associations, we see both his eye for detail, and the aphoristic edge discussed earlier working to great effect. In 'The Submerged Bar' (part of 'The Unlit Suburbs' sequence) we encounter a dream-like utopic bar, where 'the drinks are all self-serve/and the last bell's never rung'. The poem ends with 'and no policemen comes knocking/in the middle of the night/but it's best not to be found there/during the hours of daylight'. The piece is neatly tied up with an ambiguity of whether this is a dream, or reality, but the reader doesn't feel cheated of resolution, once again, the tone of the poem is consistent, and the ending is delicately phrased.

Throughout *The Night Post*, my opinion of Sweeney's work has been constantly shifting from admiration to confusion. The best pieces of the book carry a dark undercurrent of dream, fantasy, and taboo, the poet exploring them in precise detail, revealing them to be made new again, the poet himself describing it as 'imagistic narrative'[1]. However, in the more mundane-based content of the book, there is a real lack of innovation and originality of word-choice that made

---

1 http://lidiavianu.scriptmania.com/Matthew%20Sweeney.htm (First accessed 10/12/10, Last accessed 13/12/10)

me consider whether this was written by the same poet. It is a work of mixed quality, and it will be down to each individual reader to decide whether the low-impact poems are worth trudging through to find the stark and wonderfully explorative pieces that they alternate with.

Dan Sluman

Rootling: New and Selected Poems
Katie Donovan
Bloodaxe, £10.95

Katie Donovan's latest collection of poetry, 'Rootling', contains new work as well as selected poems from previous collections. The title of the book is striking and beautifully apt. The organic dynamism of the verb 'rootling' brilliantly encapsulates the title poem's conjuring act, of transforming the striking physicality of the image of a baby rooting for its mother's breast when nursing - 'Little wrester, /you snort, snuffle/and lunge; /latching on/like a cat/snatching and worrying her prey' - into a humorous feminist reimagining of the iconic mother and baby image.

Donovan is one of several prominent poets forming part of a vibrant surge of new Irish and Northern Irish poetry. The recent poetry anthology, *Identity Parade*, edited by Roddy Lumsden, has further contributed to drawing attention to the riches of contemporary Irish and British verse. Donovan's poetry is grounded in her contemporary Irish context, even when the setting is further afield. When using the physical or symbolic dimensions of setting in her poem, she succeeds in pushing beyond the immediate, drawing intelligent and moving parallels between the wider world and Irish realities. In her annotations to the poem 'The Wave', Donovan explains that the poem is about the murder of an 11-year-old boy from Midleton. The boy was killed by a neighbour, and his disappearance coincided with the tsunami catastrophe. Drawing together such individual and collective experiences of trauma, Donovan powerfully evokes grief in an uncluttered way which makes the impact all the more devastatingly poignant. 'You Meet Yourself' similarly connects feelings of alienation and homecoming, America and Ireland, in its theme of encounters. As a genre, travel writing is quite a mixed bag, consisting of differing discursive approaches to writing, poetry being a form less commonly used. This makes Donovan's poems about journeying and encounters between self and other all the more exciting and innovative.

Donovan's poems reflect a political awareness, in her treatment of the topic of Irish history. The pensive, quietly angry poem 'Hunger at Doolough' reflects on the Doolough tragedy during the great Irish famine in 1849: 'The black lake is full of skeletons, /from the hundreds who trod the famine walk, /knocked on the door of the big house, /and were turned away.' The poem draws connections between an oppressive past history and the present-day threat to natural resources posed by capitalist exploitation in the form of gold mining, thus facilitating an individual and collective process of reconnecting with a poignant history of oppression: 'they'll feed/the hungry claw/of the strip-mining company, /come to scratch/for gold [...] but biting in and quaffing down, /we find only the bitter taste/of greed'. 'Bookey's Bridge, The Harrow, Wexford, 1798' is another fine poem which takes its starting-point in Irish history of conflict: 'You can speak of bridges, /of burning and hanging, /of building again, /and meeting in the centre/to shake hands'. Donovan's endnote explains that the bridge referenced in this poem is: 'where the first confrontation of the 1798 Rebellion in Ireland took place'. Irish mythology and oral narrative traditions are also drawn on, in the evocation of physical and spiritual dimensions in the sheelana-gig of 'Gobnait's Shrine', and in the revisionist mythmaking of 'Macha's Curse': 'Whenever strangers come/to fight you/for your land,/you'll find yourselves/cast down by the pangs/of a woman/in her labour,/and then you'll know/what your bets and boasts/have done to me this day.' In the latter poem, the tone and vocabulary emulates a folk tale or folk song, re-imagining this ancient tale of female authority and strength.

Among Donovan's finest poems are those which evoke experiences of mothering; this is really important, powerful, work which celebrates the physicality of relationships with humour, and emotional authenticity. Donovan carefully depicts the growth of her other creations – her children – and of herself as a poet and person, in the process of mothering. 'The Things I Do For You', is a dizzy happy love song addressed to her small daughter: 'Girl, I am stretched beyond myself/like a tree that is bent so far in a sea wind/It is almost drowned. / The gate I close on my private garden/only you, with your deft hands can open, tear off its hinges and force me to gladness'. However, having a baby is no fairy-tale, and the story of the journey towards motherhood is far from straightforward, as the poem '11 Week Scan' reveals. This poem explores the agonising and difficult decisions which the speaker/mother may be asked to make, as she faces up to the possibility of loss, she finds the tenacity of the growing baby boy in her womb, who has his own agenda, and, finally, her relief when test results are declared 'normal'; 'At 41 I'm supposed to be too old/for the comfort of expecting/a normal child'. Donovan's accomplished poems on motherhood reflect a sense of discovery, of self and other, of the unexpected, of the pangs and beauty of relationships. Other poems explore issues at other end of the spectrum. She reflects on illness and old age, in the symbolic act of 'Carrying My Father up the Stairs', the mourning of an ageing pet cat in 'Tia', and of loss in 'Quietly' and 'How High a Tree Could Be'. In 'Back to Us', the speaker depicts her partner's recuperation from surgery. These are subjects at the core of human experience, made poignantly luminous by Donovan's assured touch and uncluttered poetic language.

Rootling: New and Selected Poems spans almost 2 decades, and includes work from Donovan's previous Bloodaxe poetry collections *Watermelon Man* (1993), *Entering the Mare* (1997), and *Day of the Dead* (2002). This inclusivity enables the reader to get a sense of Donovan's poetic development and creative range. It is exciting having been granted the privilege of observing the growth of an artist in this way.

Dr Charlotte Beyer

Ten New Poets: Spread the Word
Bernadine Evaristo and Daljit Nagra (Eds.)
Bloodaxe, £8.95

Published in 2010, the Bloodaxe anthology *Ten New Poets* showcases 10 emergent voices in contemporary British poetry. The anthology arose from a report on under-representation of black and Asian poetry in British publishing. The report, cited in Evaristo's excellent introduction, 'Why It Matters', asked 'could the ogre of institutionalised racism be at work in poetry publishing?' (p13) The overarching concept of this anthology seeks to redress this absence. It is gratifying to see publishers willing to take risks in representing a multicultural British literary landscape. The book's beautiful and intriguing cover does justice to the rich tapestry of diverse poetic voices inside. The cover is based on a painting from 2002-3, called 'Afro Jezebel' by Chris Ofili. The eclectic materials used reflect the irreverent spirit of this poetry collection. The editors, Bernadine Evaristo and Daljit Nagra, are themselves representative of that diversity. Evaristo's work spans both poetry and fiction, with her 1997 debut novel-in-verse *Lara* heralding a bold willingness to take artistic risks, while Nagra was widely praised for his recent poetry collection *Look We Have Coming to Dover!*. They are themselves indicative of the pedigree involved in the making of this anthology, as are the 'bigger' names providing the introductory Comments to each of the poets featured.

From backgrounds both postcolonial and diasporic - Trinidad and Tobago, Grenada, Saudi Arabia, Bangladesh, Ireland, to name a few - the writers featured in *Ten New Poets* eloquently illustrate the changes in conceptions of British identity and literature in the last thirty years or so. Their work is indicative of a shift, towards an acknowledgement and celebration of multiculturalism in British literature. One of the most distinctive contributions to British literature has been the emergence of black British, Asian writers, diasporic, and migrant writing. These emergent writers challenge and change received 'mainstream' notions of nationality and literary tradition, and render visible the multicultural quality of British poetic expression today. The diversity of poetic approaches and styles in this anthology is challenging, but really exciting. If anything, the short sections of poetry leave the reader wanting more, and also wanting to know more – about the literary and cultural traditions which their works emerge from, and about their relationship to the language they are writing in, processes of linguistic mediation, and so on.

Black British poet Karen McCarthy Woolf's work was one of my favourite parts of the anthology. Her poignant poems evoke maternal affect, addressing such difficult and emotive subjects as stillbirth and grief. They gave the sense of a distinctive and questioning voice coming into its own. I was moved by the authenticity, as well as the technical control, of McCarthy Woolf's poetry. Born in Canada, of Saudi Arabia and Irish descent, another promising poet, Rowyda Amin, explores ideas of origin and familial relations; in the couplets of 'Desert Sunflowers'; in the dark suggestive discourse of 'Mojave', and in the complex mother-daughter relationship which forms the context of 'Monkey Daughter'. The poems are written 'with concise, cadenced rhythm, and a surefooted appreciation of how the poem's structure can support and enhance its theme' (p32). Mir Mahfuz Ali, a writer with Bangladeshi roots, demonstrates the potential that political poetry has to affect the reader. His poems bear witness to individual and collective experiences of trauma and atrocity. In his poems 'My Salma' and 'Midnight, Dhaka, 25 March 1971', poetry becomes a means of resisting oppression and reclaiming language.

Denise Saul is a black British writer from a diasporic background, her calm, controlled poems evoking both sensual and elemental realms. Roger Robinson, a poet originally from Trinidad, also reflects a diasporic consciousness through his use of memory, which sees personal and collective histories merge into brilliant snapshots like the poem 'The Standpipe'. This poem evokes an emotional and intuitive connection with self and past in the speaker, through the fluidity of the element of water. The image of the standpipe itself is indicative of the social and cultural conditions, a shared experience of deprivation. The poetry of Shazea Quraishi is influenced by her work as a translator. Her poem, 'The Courtesan's reply', is 'inspired by Manomohan Ghosh's translations from the Sanskrit of *The Caturbhani*', as Stephen Knight notes in his introductory Comments (p72). Malika Booker uses imagery from slavery to insist on the part poetry plays, in the confrontation with individual and collective histories, and the creative re-visioning of self.

Seni Seneviratne's poetry reflects a fascination with the nuances of literary language. 'Sitting for the Mistress' employs an actual painting, the Portrait of Louise Keroualle, Duchess of Portsmouth, French Mistress of Charles II, posing with her black child servant, Pierre Mignard, 1682, currently hanging in the National Portrait gallery, as a starting-point for an exploration of margins and centre. Seneviratne brilliantly re-imagines the painting from the point of view of the marginalised black child servant. Using the imagery of a blackbird seeking liberation, the poem powerfully illustrates the revisionary capacity of poetry, as it challenges received white Anglocentric master narratives. Nick Makoha was born in Uganda, and his traumatic history is reflected in his powerful writing as it 'deals with displacement, loneliness and the impact of forced exile'. Janet Kofi-Tsekpo, an exciting prose and poetry writer, demonstrates subtlety and imaginative richness in the pensive 'Poem for Rumi' and 'Book of Puddle'.

As the editors explain, this anthology is the result of an initiative by the literature development agency, called Spread the Word. This work deserves widespread support, just as this anthology deserves a wide and questioning readership. *Ten New Poets* gives a welcome 'nudge' to the literary and critical establishment to open its ears to the new voices in British poetry today.

Dr Charlotte Beyer

Night
David Harsent
Faber & Faber, £9.99

The majority of the poems in *Night*, David Harsent's tenth collection, capture the subconscious landscape of events and inner dialogue that takes place in dreams or in the moments before sleep overtakes wakefulness.

> ...'The edge
> of night.... those forms that catch and hold
> just at the brink where it's nearly but not quite.'
> (The Hut in Question)

Harsent manages to 'catch and hold' these forms so that they are recognisable but without losing the mystery of the subconscious.

There are a few short poems but mostly narratives unfold in longer works. Themes are also developed and revisited in poem sequences and in, as Harsent terms them, 'suites' of poems such as the five poems commissioned by Radio 3's *The Verb* which are interspersed throughout the collection, with each poem concerning a different use of the word 'Blood.'

For me the engine of all Harsent's poems is their musicality. Rhyme and rhythm both drive and lead narrator and reader from line to line. Harsent has no fear of repetition whether of sounds or words. While the collection is entitled 'Night' with many poems occurring between dusk and dawn, my guess is the word 'light' appears in the majority of poems and other words such as 'touch', 'hand' and 'blind,' act as touchstones throughout the collection. Just as when looking into a kaleidoscope you see the same coloured beads but in infinite different patterns, so Harsent's repetition gives both a familiarity and an alteration in a word's meaning and context. 'The Garden in Sunlight' starts by using the repetition of 'white' in concrete images:

> 'Go by white poppies, white tulips, white flags, go by

the white willow arch, go by the apple tree, its full white crop,

go by the pond where white-eyed fish
slide by deeper each day,'

Yet soon you are 'adrift in white's slow creep/away and over the edge' and by the end of the poem maintaining a concrete existence is impossible:

'...it's white on white however hard you try,

and a hum in the air, white noise, which could be some rash
report of you: figment, divertimento, little white lie.'

I've always admired Harsent's use of rhyme. Usually there is no regular rhyme scheme with often a rhyme sound first appearing as a couplet and then being woven in with other rhymes, always reappearing just before the sound fades from your aural memory. Sounds reappear as internal rhymes as well which alters the rhythm and adds momentum to the work. 'Moppet,' a short poem of ten lines is dominated by one rhyme although other sounds and alliteration weave through it:

'Consider the rip for a mouth, the rip in the crotch, the hank of hair,
consider the flair for ill-fortune, the empty stare, the done deal
with sorrow, the rich and rare nest egg of dreams, the share and share
alike in matters of loss,...'

My impression is that Harsent constantly opens up new directions and take off points for the narrative of a poem, by working with rhyme in this way. A recent interview for a Faber podcast with George Miller where Harsent described creating poems through; 'taking a line for a walk' backs this up. Improvising from a line, however skilfully done, could end up as a fascinating technical exercise for the poet but a soulless post modern jaunt for the reader. There's no danger of this happening in *Night* with its compelling narratives and breathtaking lines like 'Imagine a shred of song drawn through a blown egg, think/ of a whisper held in an empty house...' Harsent also described in the interview his excitement when: 'you get to the point where you can see what you're up to' and his ability to tune and shape a poem at this point is equally skilful.

This way of creating is also mirrored in the content of *Night* with many of the narrators in the poems appearing to have reached a place in time from which there is no map or known destination. 'Rota Fortuna', the opening poem, sets out the possibilities:

'...no way to know what's next, what sleight
of hand those hags might bring to the game, or why
it's you at all, or whether the black and white,

the yin and yang, that ever-turning wheel, its rote:
I rise, I rule, I fall, and *I am crushed,*
will play out in your favour.

This wheel of fortune is one of several themes explored in this book. Many poems are journeys through a narrator's internal and external world, with death and reckoning present in many guises. There are three Cavafy versions here but the Cavafy poem I kept seeing parallels with was 'Ithaca,' (it is mentioned in 'The Duffel Bag') where journey is exhorted over destination.

Each time I reread the poems more layers and themes were revealed. I found the same with 'Legion' Harsent's previous collection, however some of the war poems in that collection were more accessible and therefore hard hitting on a first reading. This was partly because they were reflecting the events in Afghanistan and Iraq that were being reported in the media at the time. In many ways the strength of *Night* though is its ability to make the intangible recognisable without making it tangible.

In the podcast Harsent discussed the many possible meanings of the word 'white,' explored in the poem 'The Garden in Sunlight' which I quoted from earlier. He felt 'white' also connected with 'not being able to find the edge of things.' In poetry the poet reveals edges that readers don't often see or realise are present. In doing this the reader gets a fresh idea of the shape and form of something. In 'Night' Harsent brings to light those vanishing points where the edges are about to be either lost or found and so charts the strange but ultimately familiar logic of dreams and the subconscious.

George Miller interview with David Harsent http://www.faber.co.uk/podcast/

Sally Clark

The Patron Saint of School Girls
Liz Berry
the tall-lighthouse, £5.00

Liz Berry was a bright and engaging reader of her poetry at the 2009 Ledbury Poetry festival. So I am delighted to find that her poems speak as strongly from the page when the reader doesn't have the benefit of her voice to express them.

Berry is adept at tapping into the voice of her heritage, with poems here about the dialect and history of the Black Country, but she is also capable of throwing her voice and speaking in many guises.

The common thread throughout these poems is that the characters that inhabit them are shape shifters whose identities, gender and species are never fixed. From the opening poem, 'When I was a boy' starting with the lines: 'I was a boy every week day afternoon / when I was seven,' through the title poem where a school girl charts her metamorphosis into a saint, through poems where the animal in the human emerges - a dead lover returning for his beloved as a dog, an owl taking on whatever form necessary to wreak revenge, 'I carried curses / between my claws, drought in my beak.' What comes across is both a fascination with the distinct identities that take shape and an exposure of a communal identity, the primordial soup bubbling beneath the surface in all of us. In the fug of 'In the Steam Room' Berry describes how '...shapes shift, / and we are all vapour / scorch breathed and boundary less' and ultimately how their bodies dissolve back through birth, to conception:

> 'cells loosening and yielding in the heat,
>   slackening
> into pleasure
>   deeper
>   then deeper
>   to that bodiless moment

where atoms met

and life gasped

I'm coming, I'm coming

in the darkness.'

There is a dark humour in many of these poems but Berry's voice has a straightforward, innocent quality to it with poems often ending on a transcendent note. The narrative never descends into syrupiness, because it is juxtaposed with an animality, a baseness. 'Fir' for example, a poem about a couple bringing home and setting up a Christmas tree, contains the gentle image of the lights strung on the tree creating an 'aurora borealis in the dark of the living room.' However the first line of the poem addressed to the tree: 'You brought the wild into our house' has already forewarned us of another dimension and by the end of the poem the couple are lost in the 'feral stink of pelt':

'We were down on all fours , rolling like wolves
as you closed in around us, whispering, whispering.'

Coming from the Midlands myself I also appreciated Berry's descriptions of the Black Country where she was born, with communities, characters and dialects, such as in 'Homing' with 'vowels ferrous as nails, consonants // you could lick the coal from'.   Her sadness at seeing this rich heritage disappearing makes for more than merely nostalgic poems where history is neatly parcelled as memory and hearsay. Instead within the humour and arresting images is an acknowledgement of how this past continues to echo and shape her present. As in the closing stanza of 'Goodnight Irene':

'When you were a girl, those streets shone
like the coal, traipsing home with your dad from the pit's
black skeleton, your hand in his pocket, close as a kiss.
Now their names are like music, a requiem:
Darkly Lane, Snow Hill, Roseville, Wren's Nest.'

What impresses me most about this pamphlet is the evenness of the poems. There are no poems that grab your attention with a striking opening line, then fall short of maintaining interest through the body of the poem before resuscitating themselves with a hefty punch line.   Berry's poems consistently serve up interesting metaphors and images, drawing you forward from line to line. I'm very much looking forward to seeing this sustained in a full collection.

Sally Clark

Chickweed Wintergreen: Selected Poems
Harry Martinson, translated by Robin Fulton
Bloodaxe, £10.95

In 1920, aged 16, Harry Martinson ran away to sea. It may have been the last time he allowed anything approaching a cliché into his life. Seven years later a lung condition forced his return. So began one of the century's most unusual literary careers.

The outline is impressive enough. Martinson published eleven volumes of poetry between 1929 and 1973, the last appearing five years before his death. He also published four novels: the autobiographical novel *Nässlorna blomma* (Flowering Nettles) remains among the classic Swedish accounts of childhood; *Vägen till Klockrike* (The Road to Klockrike) is a philosophical account of the failure of a group of tramps to adapt to the industrialised world (Martinson himself had experience of sleeping rough and, aged 21, had been arrested for vagrancy). There were also six volumes of essays and a number of plays. In 1949 he was elected to the Swedish Academy; in 1974 he won the Nobel Prize for Literature.

But the outline tells only half the story. Martinson was never the establishment figure that this list of achievements suggests. His style was under almost constant review; he seems to have delighted in defying people's expectations of him.

Right from the start, Martinson was recognised as – in that overused term – a new voice. A herald of Swedish modernism, and part of a group of young, working class writers, his early work disturbed some readers. "His texts were full of exotic geography, rough living and hard-bought knowledge, raw sensitivity – all suggested in shimmering language, swirling light-footed metaphors, deep playfulness", says Staffan Söderblom in his intelligent and sensitive introduction.

If this suggests Martinson was one of those writers who decorate their work with a veneer of exoticism – borrowings from 'darkest Africa' or the 'mysterious East' to titillate the jaded Western palate – it shouldn't. What comes across most from the early poems in *Spökskepp* (Ghost Ships) is the author's dispassionate confrontation with life's grime and hardship. It is "so packed with concrete details, so rough in a way, that it has the authenticity of the world itself... it is fundamentally matter-of-fact" says Söderblom of the poem 'Have you seen a steam collier...':

> Have you seen a steam collier come from a hurricane –
> broken booms, wrenched railings,
> dented, wheezing, done in –
> and a captain quite hoarse?

Similarly, 'Cable-ship' from 1931's *Modern Lyrik* (Modern Poetry) describes the arduous process of repairing transatlantic cables: "When we put our ears to the gnawed part / we heard the murmuring in the cable. / One of us said: 'It's the millionaires in Montreal and St John's / discussing the price of Cuban sugar / and the lowering of our wages'."

Already, though, Martinson's themes were developing. Poems of the sea, work and hardship mingled with poems of home and the country. In time – with the collections *Nomad* (1931), *Nature* (1934) and *Cicada* (1953) – he was to establish himself as perhaps the country's premier chronicler of a rural Sweden that was already in retreat. Again, though, his poems are a long way from straightforward celebration. Martinson's countryside was always faintly menacing; nature is an alien place where people no longer belong. In 'Near the Sea', for example, from *Nomad*, an agricultural implement becomes something from a folk tale:

> In the all-in-one shadow of the aspens
> a horse-drawn rake is sunk
>   wheels drowned in grass
> and where its long witch-teeth bite the turf
>   a pennycress has blossomed.

In 'Autumn', meanwhile, from *Nature,* a farmer is depicted almost attacking his fields: "The plough makes autumn's first black rip in the yellow stubble / widens its morning wedge to a day's dark rectangle, / bigger and bigger until muffled in dusk".

There are wonderful moments of sideways observation, too. In 'The Midge-catcher', for example, a bat "cut sideways though the mist / like half a tiny black umbrella / then opened out and hovered", while the berries on 'The Juniper Bush' "sit in clusters / like intercepted shotgun pellets."

Martinson's later work is marked, according to Söderblom, by "his deepening disquiet about contemporary life: the mechanisation of landscape, the poisoning of air and water". The oddest, most mould-breaking work of this period has to be *Aniara.* Published in 1956, it is best described as a dystopic exercise in science fiction poetry. 103 'songs' tell the story of a spaceship carrying survivors from a doomed earth that is knocked off course by a comet and sent hurtling into deep space, while its human occupants struggle to cope with or hide from their fate. The ship becomes a metaphor for a civilisation that Martinson could no longer condone.

Certainly, as Söderblom notes, the poems that follow *Aniara* portray a constant theme of loss. 'The Shadows', for example, from *Vägnen* (The Carriage, 1960) is a powerful meditation on sorrow: "since the sap counted the possible growth rings / a sorrow drew a stroke of its bow through the world." Similarly, 'The Last Load' from 1971's *Poems on Light and Darkness* is one of a number that reflect on the destruction of a rural way of life. I include it here in full:

The last harvest load creaked home.
The fields lay stubby and chill.
An old woman straggled after, distressed
by all that had no chance of staying.

But there is also much more – an ongoing interest in nature, in ancient history and Eastern thought in particular – that make these poems a bittersweet pleasure.

After criticism of his award of the Nobel prize, Harry Martinson attempted suicide. He failed, but instead turned his back on literature, writing nothing else after 1974. Still well loved in his native Sweden, his reputation declined elsewhere. Hopefully Robin Fulton's assured translations, and this generous selection, will introduce his work to a new generation of English readers.

Ross Cogan

Poetry Contributors
in order of appearance

Jane Commane was born in Coventry in 1983. She is Co-editor of Nine Arches Press and *Under the Radar* magazine, as well as a workshop tutor. She lives in Warwickshire and is working on a debut collection of poems.

Owen Gallagher is from Gorbals, Glasgow and lives in London. His poetry collections include: *Sat Guru Snowman* and *Peterloo Poets*. *A Good Enough Love* is forthcoming from Salmon Poetry, Ireland, June 2011.

Charlotte Gann lives in Sussex. She is a writer and editor, with an MA in Creative Writing and Personal Development. She has had poems in *The Rialto*, *The North* and *Magma*, among others, and her first pamphlet, *The Long Woman*, is published by Pighog.

Ian McEwen studied philosophy and then worked in investment banking before returning to writing in 2002. Magazines his poems have appeared in include *Smiths Knoll*, *Poetry Wales* and *Poetry Review*. He is on the board of *Magma*. His pamphlet *The Stammering Man* was a winner in the Templar competition 2010.

Liz Bahs is working on a Creative Writing PhD at Royal Holloway, University of London, supervised by Jo Shapcott. She teaches creative writing for University of Sussex and The Open University. Her poetry has been published in a variety of magazines and she is working on her first collection, *Swarm*.

Luigi Coppola is an English teacher in London, trying to instill as much enjoyment of literature, and especially poetry, in his pupils as possible. Currently working towards a first collection having studied English & Creative Writing at Warwick University.

Marion Tracy has spent the last six years in New South Wales and now lives in Brighton. She's had work in, *Obsessed with Pipework*, *The Rialto*, *14 Magazine*, *Mslexia* and *Tears in the fence* and is extensively published in Australia. She has a pamphlet forthcoming with Happenstance next year and a profile on poetry pf.

Roy Marshall was born in 1966. After a variety of jobs he trained to be a nurse. Roy has had work accepted by The *Rialto, Staple, Smiths Knoll* and other magazines. His first pamphlet will be published in 2012.

Denise Bennett has an MA in creative writing. Her work has been widely published. She has pamphlet collection *American Dresses,* by Flarestack and in 2004 she won the inaugural Hamish Canham poetry prize. Her first collection *Planting The Snow Queen* will be published by Oversteps this year.

Michael Curtis *Walking Water,* an English/French sequence by Editions des Vanneux, was published in 2009 and *Melnais suns*, Latvian translations of his poetry and prose, was published in 2010. He recently read in Munich and next autumn will be in residence at French regional capital of culture, Béthune, for Poésie et Gastronomies. Meanwhile he is collaborating on a series of seasonal Poems by Post with artists in Charente.

Sarah Davies is originally from Merseyside, and wanted to be a poet from a young age. After a long break, she started writing again in her 30s, has had work published in several magazines and is putting together her first pamphlet.

David Duncombe lives in Derbyshire. He has four collections of poetry as well as poems published in numerous magazines and has won several prizes. He was awarded a Hawthornden Fellowship. He has also written novels for children and has had drama and short stories broadcast on BBC radio.

Margaret Wilmot was born in California. She has lived in Sussex since 1978. Her poems have been published in *Scintilla, Acumen, Smiths Knoll, Rialto, Magma, Poetry Nottinghm, Iota, Temenos, The Frogmore Papers, Quattrocento, Staple, Connections, Artemis, Assent*, and the *North* as well as in various anthologies.

F.J.Williams was born in Liverpool and studied English at Durham. He taught in schools and lectured in English at University College Chester. He has two collections, *Reading Lesson in the Lifers' Wing* (Peterloo 2009) and *The Model Shop* (Waterloo 2011). He is a writer and reviewer living in the North West.

Helen Reid has lived in Oxford for the last five years and have recently completed the University of Oxford Undergraduate Diploma in Creative Writing. Her fiction has been published in Mslexia magazine. Helen will be performing with the Morning After Poets as part of Oxfringe 2011.

Jonathan Edwards is the winner of an Academi new writer's bursary and the Terry Hetherington Award. His work has appeared in a range of magazines, including *Magma, Poetry Wales* and *The Rialto.*

Sharon Black is originally from Glasgow but now lives in the remote Cévennes mountains of southern France. She has been published in various magazines including *Mslexia, Envoi* and *Orbis* and has won several poetry prizes. Her first full poetry collection, *To Know Bedrock*, will be published by Pindrop Press later this year.

Robin MacKenzie teaches French at St Andrews University. His poems have been published in a number of magazines, in the UK and abroad, and in the anthology *Stolen Weather* (Castle House Books), edited by Karsten Piper and Douglas Dunn.

Caroline Natzler has been published in many poetry journals. Her collections are

Design Fault (Flambard Press 2001), work from which was highly commended in the Forward Prize nominations, and *Smart Dust* (Grenadine Press 2009). She hopes to complete a third collection soon. Caroline teaches creative writing in London which she finds rewarding and rather easier than actually writing!

Jake Campbell is a 22 year old writer from South Shields. Having completed an MA in Creative Writing at the University of Chester, he is currently working on the manuscript for a long poem which explores the vacillations in landscape and memory that underwrite his experiences of Tyne and Wear.

Eluned Rees's previous occupations range from dry-stone waller to psychotherapist, working for the police and NHS. She went travelling when the kids left home, returning to do an MA in creative writing at Bath Spa, then training as a hypnotherapist. She is currently renovating a cottage in Pembrokeshire.

Michael Curtis *Walking Water,* an English/French sequence by Editions des Vanneux, was published in 2009 and *Melnais suns*, Latvian translations of his poetry and prose, was published in 2010. He recently read in Munich and next autumn will be in residence at French regional capital of culture, Béthune, for Poésie et Gastronomies. Meanwhile he is collaborating on a series of seasonal Poems by Post with artists in Charente.

Sarah Davies is originally from Merseyside, and wanted to be a poet from a young age. After a long break, she started writing again in her 30s, has had work published in several magazines and is putting together her first pamphlet.

David Duncombe lives in Derbyshire. He has four collections of poetry as well as poems published in numerous magazines and has won several prizes. He was awarded a Hawthornden Fellowship. He has also written novels for children and has had drama and short stories broadcast on BBC radio.

Margaret Wilmot was born in California. She has lived in Sussex since 1978. Her poems have been published in *Scintilla, Acumen, Smiths Knoll, Rialto, Magma, Poetry Nottinghm, Iota, Temenos, The Frogmore Papers, Quattrocento, Staple, Connections, Artemis, Assent*, and the *North* as well as in various anthologies.

F.J. Williams was born in Liverpool and studied English at Durham. He taught in schools and lectured in English at University College Chester. He has two collections, *Reading Lesson in the Lifers' Wing* (Peterloo 2009) and *The Model Shop* (Waterloo 2011). He is a writer and reviewer living in the North West.

Helen Reid has lived in Oxford for the last five years and have recently completed the University of Oxford Undergraduate Diploma in Creative Writing. Her fiction has been published in Mslexia magazine. Helen will be performing with the Morning After Poets as part of Oxfringe 2011.

Jonathan Edwards is the winner of an Academi new writer's bursary and the Terry Hetherington Award. His work has appeared in a range of magazines, including *Magma, Poetry Wales* and *The Rialto.*

Sharon Black is originally from Glasgow but now lives in the remote Cévennes mountains of southern France. She has been published in various magazines including *Mslexia, Envoi* and *Orbis* and has won several poetry prizes. Her first full poetry collection, *To Know Bedrock*, will be published by Pindrop Press later this year.

Robin MacKenzie teaches French at St Andrews University. His poems have been published in a number of magazines, in the UK and abroad, and in the anthology *Stolen Weather* (Castle House Books), edited by Karsten Piper and Douglas Dunn.

Caroline Natzler has been published in many poetry journals. Her collections are

Design Fault (Flambard Press 2001), work from which was highly commended in the Forward Prize nominations, and *Smart Dust* (Grenadine Press 2009). She hopes to complete a third collection soon. Caroline teaches creative writing in London which she finds rewarding and rather easier than actually writing!

Jake Campbell is a 22 year old writer from South Shields. Having completed an MA in Creative Writing at the University of Chester, he is currently working on the manuscript for a long poem which explores the vacillations in landscape and memory that underwrite his experiences of Tyne and Wear.

Eluned Rees's previous occupations range from dry-stone waller to psychotherapist, working for the police and NHS. She went travelling when the kids left home, returning to do an MA in creative writing at Bath Spa, then training as a hypnotherapist. She is currently renovating a cottage in Pembrokeshire.